It'll Be All Wrong On The Night

Reginald Frary has sung in his local church choir in Richmond, Surrey for more than fifty years. The peculiar world of draughty vestries, tyrannical organists and musty-smelling hymn books has inspired forty years of story-telling and laughter.

This is Reg's second collection of stories to be published by the Canterbury Press, and follows the deservedly popular *We Sang It Our Way*.

It'll Be All Wrong on the Night

More choral triumphs and disasters

Reginald Frary

CANTERBURY
PRESS
Norwich

© Reginald Frary 2002
Cover illustration © Paul Cox 2002

First published in 2002 by Canterbury Press Norwich
(a publishing imprint of Hymns Ancient & Modern Limited,
a registered charity)
St Mary's Works, St Mary's Plain,
Norwich, Norfolk, NR3 3BH

www.scm-canterburypress.co.uk

British Library Cataloguing in Publication data

A catalogue record of this book is available
from the British Library

ISBN 1-85311-508-8

Typeset by Rowland Phototypesetting Limited,
Bury St Edmunds, Suffolk
Printed in Great Britain by
Bookmarque, Croydon, Surrey

Dedication

To my friend Hilary Youngman, New Zealand church organist and chorister, and all who carry on the great tradition of service 'in quires and places where they sing'.

Contents

Preface

Long before Captain Mainwaring of *Dad's Army* made famous his shrivelling remark, 'You *stupid* boy,' a similar remark was constantly in use by my first choirmaster, another man who would stand no nonsense. Sing a wrong note after he had very definitely taught you how to sing the right note, fail to sing a simple scale in one breath, get lost and give up in the *Alleluia Chorus*, loll all over the choirstall, bury your head in a hymn book and mumble through 'Stand up, Stand up for Jesus' – sins like these called for an immediate reduction in your choir pay. 'Down you go – four pence', and the words of disdain, 'You *silly* little boy.'

We remained silly little boys until our voices eventually broke, and so came the day when we could leave the choir and free ourselves from the rule of the martinet. Strangely though, most of us did not go. We simply graduated to the back row of the choirstalls and became choirmen – some of us are still there in the back row in churches in many parts of the world. Throughout my boyhood years, our choirmaster, that unrepentant autocrat of the old school, had drilled and drummed into us a lasting lively appreciation of church music in all its forms and an ever uplifting pleasure in choral singing that have so greatly enriched our adult lives. His silly little boys owe his memory much.

RF
March 2002

1

Track Record

In the choir of the village church where my bachelor cousin Charlie is organist they've got a man affectionately known as Bodger, who has been there for fifty years and in all that time has never been late for a service, never missed a choir practice and never had the faintest idea of how to sing. He says he sings tenor or bass depending on how he feels at the time, and in fact always hoots the soprano melody in everything, producing an unearthly sound that has nothing to do with tenor or bass or anything above or below, and easily swamps every other sound in the choir. He is, and always has been, the most enthusiastic, dedicated member of the choir and for years has solely financed with an unbelievably lavish hand the choir's riotous Christmas Dinner event at 'The Spotted Dog' and the effervescent summer outing to Clacton. (The vicar – always dutifully invited – invariably has a pressing pastoral engagement on the outing day and sees the choir off in their coach, full of voluble regrets that once again the call of duty has robbed him of a wonderful community experience.) The entire choir enjoy these two traditional highlights of their year to such an extent that no one has ever, even obliquely, hinted to Bodger that his membership of the choir is directly responsible for the regular furious complaints about ruined choral weddings ('she looked gorgeous and the flowers were lovely – but that awful man in the choir . . .') and the choir's regular rock bottom ratings in the results of the annual music festival. As for throwing Bodger out of the choir, lock, stock and barrel, such ungrateful thoughts never surface in the minds of the members. The choir are very loyal.

Nevertheless, there arose recently what cousin Charlie referred to as a very delicate situation. It was so very delicate that choir members didn't refer to it even vaguely in the vestry or in 'The Spotted Dog' after matins. They waited till they got home from matins and 'The Spotted Dog', and immediately fell to phoning each other with a will, quite oblivious of congealing Sunday lunches and frantic dogs awaiting 'walkies'. Apparently the vicar had made an urgent, not to say desperate, appeal to the choir through Charlie to – just for once, as a special favour – fall in with his wishes about the music arrangements for a certain service shortly to take place. The vicar had a brother, a church organist of some distinction, who lived in Canada and whom he had not seen for forty years. The two had corresponded regularly but had not met because both mistrusted air travel and thought ships too slow. Now, however, the Canadian organist had made a brave decision and was flying to visit his brother in two weeks' time. He had emphasized (and he was a very emphatic musician) that he was especially concerned to meet and hear the choir of the vicar's church, and the vicar realized fearfully *that* could only mean a battery of outright, outraged criticism that would certainly upset the choir (Charlie's choir are easily upset) and abruptly leave the choirstalls empty until he could employ his well known over-the-top ecclesiastical flattery and monetary generosity in 'The Spotted Dog' in order to fill them again – a prospect he didn't really relish. Losing no time he sought out Charlie around midnight when, as was his custom, that unconventional maestro was filling the dark, empty church with mighty warlike organ strains from *The Twilight of the Gods*.

'I wonder if I could make a small suggestion,' he roared into the organist's ear in a determined effort he wouldn't understand, wouldn't appreciate, our choir's unique renderings of the hymns and psalms ... Dear Bodger is such an asset to us all in so many ways. We love him, of course. But could the choir possibly manage without him – just for this special evensong?' The tower clock struck midnight.

A hastily, secretly convened meeting of the choir (minus Bodger) took place the following evening. As it was of necessity secret, it was held, not in the choir's normal venue, the back room of the 'The Spotted Dog', but at Charlie's abode, a tiny, endearingly ramshackle stable-like affair of the type nowadays enthusiastically referred to by estate agents as a charming bijou Victorian residence. Apart from his musical interests Charlie's overriding passion is for trams – trams of every kind and every period. His dwelling bears startling evidence of this. The microscopic room, scene of the emergency choir meeting, is crammed with tram memorabilia, from two-way seats to wheels and brakes, from control handles to entire direction boards, and boxes of thousands of used tickets. From the midst of the chaos rises a complete cast-iron spiral staircase from one of the last Edinburgh trams, and over the severely congested doorway a large enamel notice from a Victorian London tram warns: DO NOT SPIT.

As I am regarded as a sort of associate member of Charlie's choir and was there anyway, I was invited to sit in on the meeting. I could have hardly sat anywhere else. The hall and kitchen, the only other spaces downstairs, were both half-buried with more and more tram history, and Charlie had said that the upstairs rooms were in the course of being transformed into a mini tram museum.

There was quite a free-for-all as choir members hunted for the best seats. Two of the girls quickly commandeered the two-way seat, dragging it from under a hefty plaster bust of some 19th-century engineer now wearing a tram driver's cap two sizes too large for it, and I saw one of our larger basses heaving a wad of yellowing transport magazines on to the inhospitable hardness of a tram wheel, and sinking down gratefully. I secured a good vantage point half-way up the spiral staircase, and other members eventually seemed content merely to lean against the walls on the spaces between 'special occasion' historic photographs of awesome looking groups of bowler-hatted and uniformed characters gathered round flag-bedecked trams and splendidly decorative street gas lamps.

Charlie wasted no time. Perched on a hefty tool box behind a board advertising tram tickets that enabled you to travel all day all over London for sixpence, he asked, 'Well, what're we going to do about it?' The bass on the tram wheel shifted uncomfortably and adjusted his wad of transport magazines. 'Bodger's *always* been in the choir,' he mused, puzzled. 'He can't suddenly *not* be in the choir – stands to reason.' 'He's coming round to see me tomorrow about his arrangements for the Clacton do,' confirmed Charlie, 'and I'm certainly not telling him he can't be in the choir on Sunday week – not for the vicar *or* his bossy musical brother.'

Our soprano soloist, a bright, glamorous girl always ready to say what she thinks, suggested excitedly, 'What about this? What about putting on some hymns and things at the last minute that Bodger doesn't know? He can't read music so he won't be able to sing 'em right away – at least not loudly, and we can drown him.' She beamed a brilliant smile. There was a short silence. Charlie leaned across the tram board like a dramatic preacher in a pulpit. He gaped pityingly at the soprano. 'Hymns and things he doesn't know?' he croaked. 'Girl, that man knew all the published hymns and everything else around here more than half a century before you were thought of! He knows the lot!'

One of the tenor gentlemen who had not been listening to what Charlie said – he never does listen to what Charlie says – had become very interested in a yellowing crumpled public notice of 1920s vintage. 'It says here that you could go out on a tram all evening for tuppence,' he announced to no one in particular. 'Those were the days!'

'We're talking about these days now,' reminded his neighbour. 'What are we going to do about Bodger?' The bass on the wheel spoke again, 'All this is the vicar's idea. What about *him* proposing his idea to Bodger?'

'Listen to him!' exclaimed a young man leaning on the wall, who sings more or less alto. 'The vicar won't stick his neck out. What's the use of being the vicar if you can't *delegate* and get someone else to stick their neck out?' The vicar only likes it when he can slap you on the back and shout 'Grand! Splendid! Great!'

Half an hour later, Charlie was obliged to call the meeting to order. Interest in the unique display of tram memorabilia had swiftly taken over from consideration of what to do about Bodger. 'We must sort this thing out,' insisted Charlie. 'Let's forget about trams for a bit.'

'If we hadn't forgotten about trams in this country years ago,' began the bass, 'public transport wouldn't be in the deplorable state it is today. Trams are the cleanest, quickest . . .' A raucous phone bell unceremoniously interrupted him. Charlie unearthed the phone and listened. The phone chatted on and on. We all listened. Charlie's face gradually assumed a beatific smile. He replaced the receiver under the spiral staircase. He beamed at us across the 'cheap fare' board. 'Grand, splendid, great. Message from the vicar! His brother can't make it. Just been asked, *begged* to take over the last-minute organization of a most prestigious music festival – great honour for him – lots of publicity – couldn't refuse.' Charlie waited till the sighs of relief expired. 'However, the maestro has not forgotten us. He still deems it important that he should hear our choir and requests that we record a typical evensong service and send it to him for his comments and guidance.'

There followed a sudden, indignant silence that even penetrated the consciousness of the tenor who never listened to what Charlie said. Without taking his eyes from a minute examination of a litter of

Victorian horse tram tickets, he enquired mildly, 'What's going on? . . .'

Charlie was seeing me off at the station. 'It's a pity the idea of recording the choir can't be entertained,' he said. 'The acoustics in our church are so bad that no recording made there would give us any credit at all. We can't send a musical expert like the vicar's brother such a dreadful impression of our choir.'

'Definitely not,' I agreed, 'especially an evensong recording.'

'Exactly,' said Charlie, 'most times the acoustics at evensong are even more deplorable than at matins.'

2

Community Spirit

The new vicar had amazed his congregation when he arrived in the parish. He had made it known that he wanted people to speak to, or at least smile at, each other when they met in church.

The congregation had put up with some odd vicars in their time, but never one who preached this kind of thing. They were used to sitting in their favourite pews and keeping themselves to themselves. One member recognized the presence of another only when they both arrived at the church door at precisely the same moment and it became absolutely necessary, in the interest of good manners (and the congregation were all very good-mannered), for one to indicate to the other that he or she should proceed first.

But apart from his extraordinary idiosyncrasy, the parish found the new vicar quite pleasant, and during the next few years, in their well-mannered way, most of them fell in with his wishes.

He built on his original ideas. Soon you were not only supposed to notice each other in church. You were supposed to be positively community-minded; that is, you were expected to turn up unfailingly at all the discussion groups, jumble sales, retreats and choir concerts which the vicar inflicted on the parish in quick succession and, if you didn't, you were considered very unChristian indeed and only fit to form the evensong congregation on cold foggy Sunday nights when all the community-minded members were at home in front of the fire, watching television.

And one of the most important of all the community-minded things you were expected to do was to partake in the Annual Firework Benefit Night. This took place, of course. on 5 November, and the idea was that you all took along a supply of fireworks to the vicarage garden, where you paid 50 pence per head towards the choirboys' summer outing fund for the privilege of sharing in the wonderful community spirit to be obtained from blundering about in the dark all over the vicar's wife's flower beds, and waving sparklers and trying to pin Catherine Wheels on oak trees, or getting choked with smoke round a smouldering mass of vicarage junk, which the vicar called the Community Festive Fire.

When I arrived for the show, the day-long down-pour of rain had slackened off considerably, and it was possible to stand about in the garden for quite a while without an umbrella before becoming soaked to the skin. I paid my 50 pence to a very old gentleman wearing a deer-stalker hat, who sat in a watchman's box at the garden gate and appeared to regard both me and my coin with the utmost suspicion. Eventually, however, he motioned me forward and barked 'Mind the wheel-barrow!' a fraction of a second after I'd fallen full length across it where it stood right in the middle of the path.

The Annual Firework Benefit Night was in full swing. A heavy pall of smoke from the festive fire hung over the whole scene, and black shapes barged about eagerly, apologizing for knocking each other down, and asking if anyone had any matches.

The flame of a cigarette lighter shot up a few inches from me and disclosed the furious face of a large, middle-aged gentleman who proceeded to light a cigar and blow the smoke straight into my face. He seemed glad that I was there.

'The vicar's gone too far this time,' he bellowed, jamming his foot on a jumping cracker which an unseen hand had just thrown at him with unerring aim. 'I'm on the church council, and I've always been against this community business of the vicar's. I mean to say, you used to be able just to go to church on Sunday and that was that, but now they don't like it unless you do things on weekdays as well!' He paused for a moment, outraged, and lighted a firework from his cigar, studying it closely in the light of a Roman Candle which had startlingly shot up between us. 'Light the blue touch paper and stand clear,' he read, even more outraged. 'I hate these things! Why can't they just make the sort you can hold in your hand? All these dangerous bangers!'

He flung the firework disgustedly into the crowd and returned to his former subject. 'Do you know, in the last few weeks I've been to three discussions on a new hymn book nobody but the vicar's mother wants – very determined woman, the vicar's mother! – three recitals of medieval music, two jumble sales and a lecture by a man who went on for hours and hours about the advantages of cremation.'

A particularly large billow of smoke from the festive fire momentarily blotted him out, and as I slipped away his voice roared after me, 'At least all those things were under cover, but this! – the vicar's gone too far this time!'

Someone had lit a large coloured flare and, in its lurid green light, I suddenly found myself surrounded by a circle of lurid green faces. One face was putting its views to the others very firmly.

'And as for standing here up to our knees in mud so that the choirboys can go on their summer outing, well, the whole thing's beyond a joke – anyway, the only place I'd like to see that lot go to would be a remand home. Biggest set of hooligans for miles!'

'I don't know,' replied another lurid green face which had been regarding curiously a very damp squib on which nearly half a box of matches had been expended unsuccessfully, 'they're not so bad, really. It's only when they start to sing that they get unbearable.'

A tremendous surge of not-so-bad choirboys and the vicar's outsize mongrel dog carved its way through the group and half-hoisted me into a sturdy bed of clinging bushes. I'm not sure what they were, but I think they must have been roses or gooseberries, because it took quite a time to disentangle my coat tails completely. There was a man next to me doing the same thing, but apparently he was also searching for his gloves, his matches and his special coloured star rocket, all of which he'd dropped when he had accidentally walked into the bushes earlier in the evening.

I offered to help him look for his belongings, but he said he'd rather carry on by himself as I might tread on his rocket, and he was determined to let it off. He said that where Firework Night was concerned he was just a great big kid and, as far as he could see, the only fly in the ointment was the vicar. He straightened himself for a moment and wiped the rain from his face.

'You'd think he'd rig up a few lights so that we could see what we're doing, wouldn't you?' he appealed. He was particularly annoyed this year because at last year's show he had walked into precisely the same bushes and lost precisely the same type of special coloured star rocket.

'The vicar's heart might be in the right place, but that's about all' he complained, as he stooped again. 'As for being remotely practical, the man's an idiot.'

And then, at last, I found myself at the *piece de resistance* of the whole show, the Community Festive Fire at the bottom of the garden. Here the vicar was in full charge and, with a dejected band of elderly gentlemen in greatcoats and bowler hats, was flinging forkfuls of sopping wet leaves and soggy cardboard cartons on to a great steaming mass, which sizzled violently and belched a solid column of yellow smoke.

'It's got a good heart in it now,' the vicar assured his audience, his wiry form forking at a tremendous pace. 'The flames will break through any moment now. Be ready to jump back, everyone – another box over here, please – and mound up at the back, gentlemen, mound up at the back. Now, have we all got forks?'

A huddled shape next to me thrust his fork into the fringe of the mass, and bent down to light a protruding back number of the parish magazine. The flame went out immediately. A grim chuckle came from deep within the huddled shape. 'That's the parish magazine all right,' he growled. 'Won't sell, and won't even burn!'

'Any moment now!' rang out the vicar's encouraging tones.

A super volcano which someone had very carefully placed in my coat pocket suddenly erupted magnificently under my left ear and then proceeded to exhaust itself over the organist, who just then appeared to be shaking the life out of a choirboy caught in the act of doing something rather thoughtless with half a dozen lighted jumping crackers and a milk bottle.

I slipped away unobserved by everyone except the suspicious gatekeeper. 'You *did* pay, didn't you?' he called threateningly, as I squelched away down the vicarage drive.

The next day was Sunday, and after evensong the whole congregation stood about in fuming and, in many cases, violently sneezing groups at the back of the church, all striving to outdo each other with heart-rending stories of what they'd endured at the Firework Benefit Night for the sake of the choir-boys' summer outing. To make matters worse, the choir had completely broken down in the anthem, and obviously hadn't known the first thing about a new hymn tune which the vicar's mother had insisted on.

The vicar strode down the centre aisle, regarding us with obvious pride. 'Splendid isn't it?' he said to me, nodding and smiling energetically at each group of dissenters. 'And yet' – and he became very confidential and drew me a little aside – 'you may not believe this, but when I first came here they all left the church *immediately* after the service, without so much as a *single word* between them.'

'It just goes to show,' I enthused.

'Community spirit!' he breathed ecstatically.

3

Refreshingly Different

I recently renewed acquaintance with a former office colleague who sings very loud bass in the choir of a battered red brick early Victorian church on a very noisy main road on the outskirts of London.

In his invitation to me to join him in the choir one Sunday, George warned that things at the church were not as I had known them ten years ago. 'These days,' he wrote, 'we have a refreshingly different vicar – description thought up and bestowed by local paper – and on Sunday mornings we have this "Happy Family" get-together sort of service . . .'

It is one of those churches where it is impossible to enter by the main door and go to your seat for the service without negotiating a solid semicircle of people just inside the doorway, all smiling at you and nodding vigorously, and competing with each other boisterously to grip your hand or clap you on the back and bellow jolly words of welcome at you. (I am reminded of those continental holiday brochures in which page after page is swamped with close-up photographs of holidaymakers all laughing hysterically or hugging each other in uncontrolled mirth – presumably because they are sprawling on a foreign beach being fried to a frazzle.)

You can, in fact, avoid the crush at the main door by entering the church by a side doorway through the verger's 'glory hole' – a tiny, chaotically crammed place of buckets, ladders, broken chairs and discarded bell ropes – that despite appearances, is infinitely easier to penetrate than the welcoming barrage at the main door.

Of course, none of this affects the choir, who have their own entrance at the choir vestry through which the entire company erupt at the very last moment before the service is due to begin. There is an excellent reason for this procedure. The organist, a musician of limitless enthusiasm and no tact at all, is always lurking in the choir vestry well before service time in the fond hope of trapping any early arrivals into taking part in an extra rehearsal of the morning's anthem. But, as George says, the choir tumbled to this crafty dodge a long time ago, and although they hold the organist in highest esteem they have enough of his bawling and stamping and generally acting like a maniac at the Friday night rehearsal, without having to put up with it all over again on Sunday morning. So the choir turn up just in time to fling on their robes and shuffle into the choirstalls, and the organist, thwarted once again, pulls out all the stops on the organ and cruelly upsets the vicar's warden, a traditionalist who is trying to compose himself for the serenity of the service. Not that the service is very serene these days. It's something made up by the refreshingly different vicar with bits from other people's experimental services and a few of his own ideas thrown in, all typed in a booklet with a fluorescent cover and peppered with drawings of groups of people gazing at an outsized sunrise. There are two or three places in the booklet recommending 'Here we may proceed as the spirit guides' when anything could happen and generally does.

Comfortably up in the choirstalls behind the chancel screen, the choir are well away from the congregational goings-on in the nave. They are not supplied with copies of the fluorescent service booklet, and would consider it none of their business anyway, their only authority being their *Hymns Ancient & Modern* and *The New Cathedral Psalter*.

The refreshingly different vicar tolerates some traditional hymns and psalms interspersed with his new 'praise songs', in acknowledgement of the choir's great usefulness in parish work. Members are first rate in tackling the many jobs in the parish that no one else wants to do. The graveyard, for instance, certainly does the choir members great credit. It is always immaculate. The verger's cat, Blunderbuss, a large round black character of infinite charm, sits around on the iron-railed tombs of the revered 19th-century military personnel and successful local tradesmen that vie with each other in size and extravagance in massive rows behind the church. Some distance from the 'parade ground', on an open grassy spot near the choir vestry doorway, is a favourite summer lounging place for Blunderbuss. It is the modest memorial slab of a man who was organist for 70 years, the grandfather of the present organist, a mere stripling who has put in only half a century's service to date. Some people – the types one finds in most parishes who are ever ready to be fussy – complain that, indeed, nothing has changed in the choir since grandfather's day, but this doesn't worry the choir, who are very proud of their traditions and anyway, as the organist points out, things *have* changed because nowadays they've got electric light and girls in the choirstalls.

But whether or not things have altered up in the choirstalls they have certainly changed down in the congregation. George says, as far as the choir are concerned the old practice remains that they process into the chancel at the beginning of the service. Then they are free to settle down to their own devices until such time as the refreshingly different vicar remembers they are up there behind the screen and announces a traditional hymn for them to sing. But for the congregation, each service is a new adventure and they don't know what's going to happen until the second the vicar lets them into the secret, so everyone has to keep alert and ready to respond at a moment's notice and not drift off into semi-consciousness like the matins congregation, or they get into a most awful muddle and lose the thread of the whole service.

On the Sunday morning that George had invited me into the choir everything started normally, and having processed into the chancel the choir settled down to their various pursuits while the vicar started his usual shouting about in the nave. As far as I could make out through the chancel screen, he was introducing the congregation to a new jolly praise song which involved a lot of bellowing, feet tapping and clapping. The glad sound increased rapidly until it became most intrusive in the choir-stalls, and then when choir members were beginning to get annoyed at their privacy being so invaded it abruptly ceased and the vicar announced a choir hymn, 'Hark the glad sound'. We hurriedly rose and sang the famous 18th-century hymn and then, thinking that was that for a while, prepared to return to our reading, discussions or contemplation of the chancel ceiling.

But on this particular Sunday *that* was definitely *not* that. George nudged me. 'This is new,' he said in a puzzled, indeed startled voice. He nodded towards the nave and I saw what was new. A small procession, headed by the vicar, were moving purposefully towards the chancel. They'd reached the choirstalls before the choir noticed them. They marched to the bottom end of the stalls by the organ and formed a semicircle around a man who was fast asleep with a copy of *The News of the World* on his lap – a revered character, the choir's oldest living bass. The vicar stood there beaming, and the ancient one's neighbour hastily dug him in the ribs and said, 'Henry, vicar wants a word.'

Henry opened his eyes, grabbed at *The News*

of the World as it slid to the floor and growled, 'Ah! . . .'

'Your birthday!' announced the vicar. 'Eighty years young today!' and handed Henry a highly coloured package and an outsized birthday card crammed with scribbled names in all directions. The vicar's party then began to clap, and the vicar waved to the congregation through the screen. They all began clapping and the choir, looking utterly bewildered, also started clapping and asking each other why they were doing that. Then the birthday bass's neighbour passed him his glasses and helped him open the highly coloured package – which proved to contain a handsome Sherlock Holmes pipe – while hurriedly interpreting Henry's immediate, incoherent bass grumblings at being awakened so arbitrarily, as a charming little speech of gratitude and warmest thanks. This seemed to please the refreshingly different vicar no end and he slapped Henry on the back and said, 'Jolly good! Splendid! Great!' and herded his party back into the nave again to continue with the family service riot.

As the choir settled again to their individual pursuits the man next to me, who had been reading a paperback entitled *Great Crimes of the Twentieth*

Century, turned to his neighbour on his other side and enquired mildly, 'What was all that about, then?' 'A new bit of the service, I suppose. You can never tell these days,' answered the neighbour, returning to his Great Crimes.

The enquirer then turned to me. 'Henry's got a *pipe* out,' he said, puzzled. 'Are they going to allow smoking at this service as well?'

'You can never tell these days,' I answered.

After the service the choir's earlier dramatic last-moment entry into the choir vestry was repeated in reverse, and I found myself being borne along in a headlong rush from the church. One of the choirgirls – whose introduction to the choirstalls together with electric light was, according to the vicar's warden, the sole enlightenment the choir had embraced in the last hundred years – told me, 'We have to get out of the way before he finishes the voluntary, otherwise he'll try to rope us in for an extra practice for tonight's anthem.'

'Perhaps your organist is a bit of a perfectionist,' I said.

'Oh, he's all right really,' she answered warmly. 'He's just got this *thing* about music, that's all.'

4

The Making of Harry

Mr friend Walter's delightful rural town (one of those full of 'much sought after properties', according to the estate agents) is served by two churches, the parish church and the daughter church.

The daughter church is a very exclusive establishment with a very superior choir. It's one of those places where the congregation from the much sought after properties are expected not to sing, but are considered highly privileged to be sung at each Sunday and at special recitals by the very superior choir. Walter explains that you can't just roll up and join the choir. You're lucky if you're even selected for an audition, and even if you get through successfully and it's subsequently revealed that you've been a member of another church choir where you've bawled hymns sung at football matches, or revel in awful Victorian anthems that sound like bawdy songs sung round a pub piano in the 1890s, your chances of acceptance are definitely dashed. In serious local music circles the daughter church's very superior choir is referred to reverently as 'pure gold'.

Down at the parish church they've got a lot of pure dross (according to the said serious local music circles). The parish church choir is much bigger than the daughter church choir, and anyone can join as long as they can really let rip with the congregation in hymns like 'Stand up, Stand up for Jesus' and 'The Battle Hymn of the Republic', and don't talk too loudly during the sermon. The parish church choir don't do special recitals but they are very good at belting out carols around the pubs at Christmas, and enjoy frequent musical celebrations for choir members who are getting married or have been in the choir for 70 years, where the singing is even more raucous than at their choral evensong.

Now one of the important events in the town calendar is Mayor Making Sunday, when the new mayor and his corporation attend choral matins in force and historical splendour, and the mayor reads the first lesson and the vicar preaches his well known enthusiastic sermon all about the wonderful Christian qualities of the caring borough council. Traditionally the service has been held at the daughter church because there is a loyal feeling that only the best is fit for such a noble borough council, and that includes the best music sung by the best choir. So, year after year the new mayor and his corporation have sat in the front three rows in dignified silence, all wearing the rapt-attention expressions reserved for such official occasions, and at the end of the service when it's time to take the collection they have been generously invited to join the very superior choir in singing one of the three hymns that the vicar is fairly certain most members of the borough council have heard of.

At the following reception the choir and organist have always been warmly congratulated on their performance, and everyone has gone home happy and relieved that once again a town event has gone off without a single hitch that the local paper could turn into a brickbat and hurl at the council.

But this year tradition has been broken. The new mayor is, among other things, the conductor of the town brass band. He is also the possessor of a huge, uninhibited bass voice which he loves to exercise as much as possible wherever he is. And he enjoys nothing better than joining with the parish church choir in their Christmas tour of the pubs. He greatly admires the parish church choir – and thus has a century of tradition been broken. The new mayor deemed that this year, his year, Mayor Making Sunday would be observed at the parish church. The vicar, being in charge of both churches, was indeed surprised but not concerned about the decision. He was, in fact, secretly pleased. His natural crusading ardour, which often manifested itself in a boisterous, utterly tuneless bellowing to the Lord, had been so often damped at the daughter church by the revered, unwritten law that ordinary mortals did not butt in when the very superior choir were singing at them. But down at the parish church you could bawl with the choir in any old way you liked because they always bawled in any old way they liked and everyone enjoyed themselves. The choir and congregation were all delighted that the new mayor was to join their vocal efforts on Mayor Making Sunday – well *nearly* everyone. The vicar's warden at the parish church really suffered. Sometimes the vicar's sermon at matins upset him and spoilt his Sunday lunch, but the choir really made him *suffer*. They were directly responsible for him writing endless letters to a like-minded friend about 'the desecration of art in our most holy place'. 'Our choir,' he wrote, 'are smothered in an impenetrable fog of debased Victorian sentimentality.' My friend Walter said the poor man was appalled, absolutely bowled over, at the new mayor's request to hold the Civic Service at the parish church, and kept on muttering things like, 'How in heaven's name do such people get into power?' and 'What are the bishops doing?' right through evensong.

Nevertheless, being a loyal parish churchman and used to saying nice things in nasty situations, the vicar's warden brought himself to say how pleased he was that the parish church choir had been granted the honour of providing and leading the music for Mayor Making Sunday for the first time in history, and Walter, being an equally loyal parish churchman, thanked him profusely for his kind words. I should say here, of course, that Walter is the organist and choirmaster at the parish church. I've known him from way back in those dear simple happy days when we were choirboys together. Walter really loved singing, particularly the gorgeous syrupy anthems and settings and hymns bequeathed to us by the Victorians – Elveys, Goss, Dykes and Stainer were his idols. Walter didn't sing merely for his choir pay; he hardly ever got any. He was fined so frequently for myriad misdemeanours, musical and otherwise (tuppence for being cheeky to the organist, fourpence for filthy boots, sixpence for bawling his head off in the quiet bits of 'Lead kindly light'), that each quarter's pay was exhausted by pay day, indeed he often went into the red and owed the church money. Consistently he caused our choirmaster more sleepless nights and twitching features than the rest of the choir and the vicar put together.

Uninvited, confusion and chaos tumbled together around him, regularly, hilariously disrupting the Friday night practices, none of which he ever missed, even when the choirmaster was not on top form to deal with him, and hoped and prayed that just for once he wouldn't turn up. To the rest of us boys he was a star, and secretly the choirmaster prized him too for he had the voice of an angel.

These days Walter raises his voice less melodiously, bawling at the well loved unruly mob that for the past 40 years have been his parish church choir.

But to return to Mayor Making Sunday. The great day for the parish church arrived bright and warm. At the back of the church the vicar's warden had seen to it that the welcoming cohort were well to the fore, wearing fadeless, eager smiles and smarter attire than for the usual Sunday matins turnout, and someone had dug out and polished some rather attractive brass collection plates (the kind that give off a betraying 'clink' when you place a coin in them instead of a bank note) to replace the usual discreet moth-eaten felt bags.

In the choir vestry Walter had reckoned that they'd better make the place a bit more worthy of the mayoral party when they trooped in after the service to congratulate the choir on their splendid performance, so one of the choirgirls quickly swept the junior choirboys' discarded sweet papers under the piano, placed a chair over the ragged corner of the venerable carpet, flicked the cobwebs from the light bulb and all was ready.

Only twenty minutes late, the Mayor and Corporation arrived, their smartly shuffling, robed procession accompanied by the mayor's brass band playing 'Colonel Bogey', and preceded by the Mayor's magnificent Rottweiler – this, Walter suggested later, to lend a bit of necessary dignity to the proceedings and hopefully attract attention away from the violently anti-traditional alderman who was sporting a baseball cap and battered trainers along with his traditional attire.

Inside the church the vicar, who didn't understand dogs and was terrified of the Rottweiler, beamed an enthusiastic welcome from behind a pew, and the rest of the committee kept on smiling and handing out hefty leather-bound 'special occasion' hymn books affectionately known in church circles as 'family bibles'. This caused a little faltering in the dignity of the affair when one or two of the frailer councillors dropped them, and when an obviously very loyal friend of the new mayor leaned out of his pew and shouted, 'Cheers, Harry! You made it', but the procession made an exemplary recovery and stumbled impressively into the reserved front pews.

Walter now gave a sort of fair-ground regal trumpeting blast on the organ to bring in the choir procession, and immediately the vicar beamed hugely at the congregation and challenged them to 'really have a go at drowning even our splendid choir' in the singing of all the hymns. We started off at breakneck speed with 'Jerusalem', backed by full organ and brass band. I couldn't hear how well the congregation responded to the vicar's challenge because 'the heavy mob' of the brass band were operating with Wagnerian splendour just behind the choirstalls, but many appeared crimson in the face and smiling breathlessly as we finished, although I did spot not a few expressions of frozen horror on the faces of the daughter church's very superior choir sitting together behind the mayoral party. Later the new mayor read the first lesson from 'The Song of Solomon' in the stentorian tones in which he upbraided the band on practice nights, and the second lesson was recited in the almost inaudible quaver of a willowy lady from the daughter church, who appeared to be so shattered that she had difficulty in standing steady at the lectern.

When we came to the sermon the vicar had become so thrilled and invigorated by the singing, in which he had joined mightily, that he gave his usual performance about the noble, caring borough council so much embellished that a party of the parish church congregation could scarce contain themselves and started applauding loudly – until the vicar's warden turned on them his freezing glare, normally solely reserved for the choir at the end of a rendering of one of their uproarious Victorian anthems.

And so the Mayor Making Service continued in its swashbuckling way, and finally came to the time for the bellowing of the last hymn when a huge collection was taken in the resurrected brass plates, which gave their rattled warning when coins were placed in them instead of bank notes. All the money was to go to the parish church organ appeal fund, so Walter was delighted. He felt it essential that he should be able to get more power from the organ to keep up with the ever growing power of his choir.

As an encore the full choir, organ and brass band combined to roar their unique thunderous version of the 'Alleluia Chorus' at the congregation, and this time the vicar's warden was powerless to stem the spontaneous, rapturous applause from the packed congregation (or at least, the parish church part of it). Finally the mayor's party started bemusedly to file from the pews. That was the end. It was all over bar the shouting.

Later that evening Walter and I were talking over a quiet supper. 'Well,' murmured Walter contemplatively, 'I don't think there will be another mayor like Harry for a long time. The next one will want his Mayor Making Service back at *their* church with *their* choir. They don't appreciate our singing, I know that lot.'

'I expect you are right,' I agreed regretfully.

Walter sighed, beamed his delightful, mischievous grin, unchanged since the days when we were choirboys together. 'But it was great, *great* while it lasted wasn't it! What a performance!'

5

In Need of Improvement

Years ago, ancient churchyards always had their accompanying ancient characters who looked after them and dug the graves. But nowadays the characters have grown so incredibly ancient that few of them are working at all and there seem to be no other characters, ancient or otherwise, to take their places. Consequently more and more vicars and church councillors are becoming worried about what to do with the churchyard.

Of course, many brilliant ideas are put forward. A favourite one is to level off the tombs, tear up the headstones and stand them round the edges of the churchyard like soldiers. The ground is thus left open and free for children to enjoy themselves playing exhilarating games and exercising their lungs to the fullest extent – particularly during service times. There is also the added attraction of a convenient area from which even the smallest child can manage to knock a ball through a church window.

Another idea is to lay down the headstones all over the place so that wherever you go in the vicinity of the church you are walking over a sort of giant crazy paving layout of pious verses and plumply etched cherubs.

Yet another brainwave is to re-arrange the churchyard entirely, with a goldfish pond and china gnomes, and another is to tarmac the lot and turn it into a car park.

But in the particular country parish which I have in mind, the ancient churchyard character was still going strong and had no intention of retiring. Indeed, his one great sorrow was that for the last few years he hadn't had an opportunity to dig any more graves because there wasn't room to get anyone else in. The trouble was that the parish had lately been saddled with a go-ahead, bright young curate who, eager to give the congregation more to do than complain about the hymns and the church's defunct heating system, had recently formed a number of Improvement Groups. These consisted of a lot of people who went around the parish upsetting a lot of other people by telling them how they should run whatever they *were* running.

There was, for instance, the Church Music Improvement Group, who painstakingly drew up exhaustive lists of music which they considered the choir *should* sing and even more exhaustive lists of music the choir *shouldn't* sing, all of which the organist received with the old-world courtesy for which he was famous, and made into spills for his pipe.

Then there was the Sunday School Improvement Group, who were full of advanced theories like letting the pupils express themselves freely and naturally by making paper bombers out of their exercise books and chasing each other about the class room, getting plenty of good, healthy exercise while the teacher talked to herself about the lesson.

There was also the Church Interior Improvement Group, whose main burning interest seemed to centre on a scheme for replacing the pews with tip-up seats, electrifying the antique gasolier, and sticking little pots of permanent plastic flowers all over the Norman pillars and the Jacobean pulpit.

And there was, of course, the Churchyard Improvement Group. This group was particularly interesting because they owed allegiance to no group leader, and were all quietly determined to carry out to the letter and at all costs their own particular improvement schemes. They all agreed that a leader would only inhibit their refreshing originality and stunt their thrilling ideas.

On the evening that I chanced to take a short cut through the churchyard the refreshing originality and thrilling ideas were in full swing. Animated figures were everywhere. On the path in front of me an eager sparrow of a man was staggering along with a tin bath filled with broken bricks and smashed fern pots which he suddenly hurled to the ground and attempted to level off with a gigantic rusty horse roller. 'No more weeds'll grow here,' he panted at me as the roller gathered momentum and threatened to add him to the new surface of the path. He grinned proudly at the chaos of crushed rubble. 'Vicar won't recognize this place when we've finished!'

I dodged round the horse roller with an encouraging smile, and immediately became fascinated by a large tweed-clad, brogue-shod lady who was smoking a cigarette in a long silver holder, and driving a cane into the ground with a coal hammer. I think the idea was to lend support to a lone hollyhock which seemed to be in a rather collapsed state.

40

The cane snapped in half under the brutish percussion of the coal hammer, and the lady lit another cigarette, produced another cane and proceeded to snap that in half also. She blew a cloud of ash and smoke at the gentleman with the weedless path. 'Devil of a job here,' she thundered. 'Ground hard as iron. Want a pick axe!'

The sparrow hurled down another bath-load of rubble. 'Worth it!' he gasped. 'Worth it!'

I picked my way forward between a group of ladies in gaily coloured smocks, who knelt beside bright little plastic buckets of foaming detergent and appeared to be scrubbing moss from a venerable tombstone depicting a rather unsympathetic gentleman with a big head and little matchstick legs forking a similar looking gentleman into a furnace.

Close by, against the churchyard wall, a tall young man with dark glasses and flaming red hair was standing contemplating a sprawling heap of rusty corrugated iron, worm-eaten planks and some battered watering cans. I sensed somehow that he might be needing some help. Perhaps the Improvement Group spirit was beginning to work for good in me also. I asked him if I could do anything.

'It's funny,' he mused without raising his eyes from the debris, 'all I wanted to do was to paint the tool shed. I couldn't do that without pulling away the weeds, could I? They were very *big* weeds and I had to pull *hard*. Fancy the whole shed falling over!'

'Perhaps it can be put up again,' I encouraged, taking off my jacket. I lifted up the corrugated roof, which promptly fell to bits and knocked down the one remaining door post. As it fell it neatly ripped my shirt down the entire length of one arm. The contemplative young man still stood there, gazing through his hair and dark glasses, but now he included my shirt in his contemplations.

'That's nasty,' he murmured. 'That's done for all right – but fancy that shed just falling over . . .'

'Well, well, what have we here? A new recruit indeed!'

I turned, and almost fell over a small bouncing young man who appeared to have in tow an adoring crowd of most attractive young ladies. He was immaculately clad in clerical grey and the very latest line in natty footwear. Even his clerical collar seemed more up-to-the-minute than other clerical collars. He consulted a notepad and then looked me up and down like a man buying a horse. I realized I was actually in the presence of the creator of the Improvement Group Movement.

He addressed his adoring band. 'A willing labourer in the vineyard with no work to do. Never let it be said.'

He nudged me along a path to a piece of open ground where a middle-aged local government officer type was gingerly picking up old tin cans and other interesting items then dropping them one by one over the wall.

'We're clearing the ground here for a Youth Club Garden,' the curate informed me briskly. 'I'll send the forks along shortly.' Then he made a tick on his notepad and bounced off at the head of his charming entourage.

The local government officer type flung a salmon tin over the wall with particular violence. 'You ought to see the *other* Youth Club garden at the back of the village hall,' he said. 'Finest crop of dandelions I've ever seen.' He gave me a conspiratorial smile. 'Did the wife get you into this? *My* wife did. All the women are crazy about *him*. She said I was letting her down in his eyes, so I had to join this lot.'

He picked up another tin and studied its label minutely. 'Rich rice pudding,' he read. 'How the dickens does rich rice pudding get into our graveyard?'

We seemed to appreciate each other. We carried on with the clearing and worked up quite an interest by organizing a little contest to see who could collect the widest variety of tins in fifteen minutes. It was a close finish. We were equal on the baked beans, condensed milk and polish, but at the last moment he unearthed a dressed crab, and of course pipped me at the post.

Then somehow we were over the other side of the wall and walking briskly down the lane.

'Come to my place and have a drink,' invited my co-deserter, adding, as he probably realized I was a little shy at bursting into the house of total strangers, 'my wife's out organizing the Village Hall Plumbing Improvement Group or something. There's only my father at home and he won't even notice you. He's very old and just sits in the kitchen laughing his head off all day.'

'A cheerful old gentleman,' I said.

His son considered for a moment. 'Well, not really,' he explained. 'Just sadistic. He's been in charge of the churchyard for forty years and reckons he's only ever had a 50 pence pay rise. He says he's going to wait till the Improvement Groups get the place into such an unholy mess that they have to come grovelling to him to put it straight again. Then he's going to be ruthless and stand our for another 50 pence.'

6

. . . Followed by Sunday School

Some years ago I used to teach in a Sunday School where you were considered a very good teacher if you succeeded in keeping the pupils from half-murdering each other for fifteen minutes at a stretch and persuaded them not to break more than two school windows every Sunday.

I was therefore rather intrigued with the speculation on what I should encounter when I recently found myself talked into taking charge of a village Sunday School class in the absence of the regular teacher, who was on holiday.

That July Sunday morning was gloriously warm and bright, and I arrived at church well before the time that Sunday School was due to start. In the churchyard a little girl with pigtails, a button nose and round red cheeks, was sitting on a tomb, tickling a monstrous tabby cat who rolled all over the place in a deliriously happy state.

'This is King Arthur,' the little girl informed me, as I paused, fascinated.

'He's the vicar's wife's baby and he does nothing but eat salmon and rice pudding.'

She could see that I was interested, and volunteered more information, rubbing her button nose reflectively and gazing proudly at King Arthur, who was now balancing on his back and sticking his feet in the air. 'He comes to Sunday School with me, but he always goes home early in case he misses his rice pudding.'

From behind the vestry two robust young gentlemen suddenly rolled. One was wielding a baseball bat with which he was endeavouring to brain the other.

'They're in the Sunday School too,' the little girl said. 'They're rather beastly.' She studied the life-and-death struggle for a few seconds. 'They're *very* beastly really,' she amended. 'None of the girls in our class is going to marry them.'

I was beginning to wonder whether I should try to act as peacemaker between these shunned males when, from behind the tombstones, the vicar loped up. He was a tall, stooping, middle-aged man with sparse fair hair. He beamed over the whole scene with an all-embracing beam. His gold-rimmed glasses shone in the sun. 'A splendid morning,' he enthused and, as the rolling young gentlemen cannoned into him, nearly knocking him off his feet, 'a morning for high spirits, indeed!'

It was said that he never spoke an unkind word about anyone – not even about members of the choir and the parochial church council. Still beaming, he invited me to come into the church to inspect my classroom. This proved to be a barn-like porch at the back of the church, curtained off from the nave by an aged green serge curtain and filled with a most interesting assortment of jumble-sale-style tables and chairs and rickety forms.

'The children all have their special seats,' the vicar explained, 'and yours is here on this little platform. Mind the third board from the left. I *think* we have just a *touch* of dry rot there. I must mention it to the church council. I think I *did* mention it to the church council last year.'

He showed me where the blackboard was kept and explained that I couldn't get at it because the verger had just stacked two ten-feet-high disused cupboards in front of it. He said that if I tried to move the cupboards they'd probably topple forward into the church and bring down the green serge curtain, which wouldn't do at all.

By this time the Sunday School pupils were beginning to filter into the porch and take their places. The little girl from the churchyard staggered in under the loudly purring bulk of King Arthur, and placed him on a battered kitchen table draped with a red velvet tablecloth. He took up a splendidly regal stance.

A number of other little girls gathered their seats around him and, at the back of the class, a knot of young gentlemen who all looked identical with the two who had been involved with the baseball bat were crushing themselves round another kitchen table, which appeared to depend on two legs, a packing case and a pile of pensioned-off *Ancient & Moderns*.

The vicar introduced me, intensified his all-embracing beam, and was gone. The lesson was on the parable of the prodigal son. From experience I had learned that, for some reason, this always commands the interest of Sunday School pupils if only you can get as far as the man eating the pigswill before they start talking louder than you can, or twisting each other's arms.

The young gentleman with the baseball bat was particularly interested. He laid his bat reverently before him on the table and concentrated on me with a sphinx-like glare. Even when, presently, a colleague behind him discreetly dropped a hairy fruit drop, discovered on the floor, down the back of his neck, he could not be drawn. He merely retrieved the fruit drop, popped it in his mouth, and remarked in tones of wonder and admiration that the prodigal must have been just like his Uncle Oscar.

'My Uncle Oscar comes to our house every Christmas,' he explained, 'and my father won't lend him any money.'

Matins was proceeding in the church simultaneously with our class, and from time to time the brutal roar of the choir enjoying themselves with a well-loved hymn came through the curtain. Leaving for a while the prodigal son merrily feasting off the fatted calf, and his respectable brother slaving away in the fields, another of the young gentlemen at the back indicated that he wished to speak with me.

'Hi! You!' he bellowed.

I was most encouraged by such obvious interest, and immediately placed myself at his disposal.

'Why can't we 'ave some singing like them in there?' he demanded. Ever ready to recruit new members, I suggested that he should apply to join the choir.

'I've been in that,' he enlightened me. 'I got chucked out.'

'The choirmaster said he was *quite* impossible,' said King Arthur's button-nosed friend primly.

'Just balmy,' corrected the wielder of the baseball bat.

A slim, elegant little girl with long straight blond hair combed over one eye, who was busy putting a nappy on a fat orange teddy bear, looked up briefly and announced, with a voice of absolute finality, 'My brother is in the choir. He gets three pounds fifty a month, and gives me a pound. He says that the choirmaster threw *him* out' – she pointed an already graceful finger at the young gentleman in question – 'because he is a moron. A moron is what he said. You can see he is a moron.'

Button Nose wrinkled her forehead and regarded me with her head on one side. 'I suppose the prodigal son was a moron,' she said slowly. 'Anyway, I don't think he was very nice.'

'He was jolly clever,' defended the ex-member of the choir. 'I bet he got some more money out of his father and went off again and had some more riotous living.'

'Crafty,' said a very small boy, whom I hadn't

noticed before. He was sitting quietly under a table, chalking faces on the soles of his shoes.

'Now for the written work,' I announced briskly. I handed out a tattered collection of exercise books, marvelling at the extraordinary names with which parents saddle their offspring these days. A quick glance through the grimy pages revealed a unique gallery of drawings depicting malformed horses, exploding atom bombs, and extraordinarily plump cross-eyed ladies, lovingly identified as 'teetcher'. Few of the books contained any attempt at written work, and this was quite understandable in the light of the teacher's red-inked remarks, which were scrawled across those pages where an attempt had been made.

'This is nonsense,' was repeated three or four times, and I also spotted a 'What *are* you talking about?', a 'Rubbish', and a 'See me'.

'May I draw a picture of the prodigal son?' asked Button Nose. 'I can do him having dinner with some pigs. They're lovely, especially the little ones.' She was already drawing a gigantic pig across one entire page.

'Yes, of course you may,' I consented.

The young gentlemen at the back were apparently having some sort of argument as to the worthiness of the prodigal. The noise began to grow alarmingly, and I was certainly very grateful to my friend with the baseball bat, who was obliged to clamber up on to the two-legged table and flourish the bat most violently before order was restored.

'He was smashing,' he declared, with great vigour. 'Cleverer than *you* lot.'

Everyone actually worked silently for at least two minutes, and then the sound of the last hymn being sung at matins was the signal for a hail of books and pencils to be aimed at my desk, and the whole class stood up with hands together in front of them.

I must have looked a little uncertain. Button Nose leaned forward confidently. 'You have to say a prayer now,' she whispered, 'then we can go.' She indicated King Arthur, who was disappearing under the serge curtain. 'He never stays for that; he goes and gets his rice pudding.'

Having cleared up the debris and rubbed out an uncannily good chalk likeness of me which had mysteriously appeared in one corner of the porch, I made my way into the churchyard. Button Nose and the elegant little girl with the blond hair were arranging the fat orange teddy bear wearing a nappy on top of a high tomb.

'And what's he doing up there?' I asked.

'He's the prodigal son's father,' explained Button Nose, 'and he's on the roof looking down the road to see if the prodigal son's coming home.'

'And what's *he* doing?' I pointed to a distinctly home-made rabbit lying face downward in a bed of nettles.

The elegant little girl glanced at him dismissively. 'Oh, he's the other son,' she said, 'slaving away in the fields while the others are having their party.'

decide that this is no good and start looking around for alternative forms of musical accompaniment. If they are lucky they may get some kind of electronic device or, if not, a new curate who plays a guitar may be pressed into service.

And, of course, all this upsets the traditional choir no end.

Something very much on these lines occurred at the church where my friend Albert is the alto soloist and choir spokesman. He told me that one or two members of the choir were talking of striking after the first Sunday without the organ, when they had to sing accompanied only by the veteran vestry piano that hadn't been played for ages. To add to the difficulties the vicar had insisted that it should be played behind a screen when brought into the chancel, because the onslaught of generations of choirboys with penknives and tendencies to vandalism had left the wreck looking quite disgraceful.

Although the majority of the choir members didn't support the idea of a strike they now sang without any of their usual enthusiasm and vigour, and didn't hold up their hymn books when singing or even pretend to be attentive during the sermon.

It was obvious that things couldn't go on like this. So on a Sunday when I happened to be visiting

Albert, the organist called a meeting of the choir in the vestry before evensong. The idea was, of course, to clarify the members' attitude to all the nonsense that had been going on, and see whether the organ couldn't be bodged up enough to be brought back into service without costing the ridiculous sum suggested by the organ builder. As Albert said, the organist really *understood* the organ and could coax almost anything out of it, even though it was falling to bits around him. But half-an-hour into the meeting we seemed to be getting nowhere with the problem, and the discussion took on a different turn, so that we found ourselves talking about Teddy, the choir's longest-serving member (seventy years' service boy and man, and no absences from a service or practice except when measles, or, in later years, the annual cricket club dinner, intervened) who was about to be honoured at a special ceremony after evensong the following Sunday.

'Fancy being in the choir for seventy years!' squeaked a pert choirgirl of some nineteen summers as the meeting broke up. 'You must get all claustrophobic – you know, panicking, wondering whether you are ever going to get out.'

'I don't think Teddy *looks* claustrophobic,'

offered a colleague arranging her well worn, rusty black choir gown to best effect over a shocking pink sequined blouse. 'He always looks sort of resigned to me.'

'Well, you have to be resigned if you want to stay in our choir for long,' agreed a solid, cheerful looking middle-aged choirman. 'First you have to be resigned to Sid (the flamboyant octogenarian organist who insists on playing Wagner grand marches at every service, from Christmas to christenings, and throughout every choir practice entreats the choir to sing "louder . . . come on . . . louder . . . let them *hear* you!"). Then there's the vicar with all her funny ideas about new jolly praise songs to replace hymns, and everybody in church acting friendly and holding up the service shaking hands and hugging each other and grinning – this "togetherness" thing. You have to get resigned to all that, otherwise you'd probably get high blood pressure – and you wouldn't enjoy being in the choir then, would you?'

At this point the vicar trotted into the vestry all briskness and encouraging smiles. She rubbed her hands together. 'Well, another big challenge to us all – to sing in tune despite the efforts of our historic piano,' she quipped. She gave a little tinkle of laughter, and despite the fact that the main obstacle to singing in tune was not the piano but the vicar's wavering voice, the choir smiled dutifully. And still holding her encouraging smile the vicar turned to the choirgirl with the shocking pink blouse and remarked how very pretty it made her look and we all processed into the chancel.

As usual the congregation were still arriving, and pushing past and falling over those who had arrived early and taken up their positions, rock-like, at the ends of pews. The choir settled into their stalls more quickly – twelve on one side and three on the other. In the distant past there had been a genuine reason why they adopted this odd balance of sides but that had long been forgotten, and nowadays the practice persisted as a revered tradition. No one wanted to change their seat or their neighbour. The same revered tradition apparently also flourished among the congregation. Some pews were crowded in the manner of a tube train at the height of the evening rush hour, while others accommodated only two or three members discreetly distanced from each other along the strip of grimly green and black seat carpet. Local folklore had it that certain pews had been the last survivors from the days of rented pews, and people were still wary of sitting in them lest the vicar demanded the rent on the way out after the service. The ornately carved, exclusive looking back pew was entered by two well camouflaged steep steps, responsible for flinging many an unsuspecting victim violently the length of the dusty floor. It was now occupied exclusively by one of those large commercial vacuum cleaners that are equipped with life-like cheerful faces, as well as by one of those vicar's wardens who are *never* equipped with life-like cheerful faces.

By the time we had got to the third verse of the opening hymn, 'Stand up, stand up for Jesus', the congregation had sorted themselves out into their chosen places, overseen by the vicar's warden who, satisfied that all was well, returned to his place next to the smiling vacuum cleaner. And then, as usual, evensong rolled along easily and pleasantly until the time came for the sermon.

The sermon is always the high point of a service at Albert's church – except, of course, with the choir, who sing at three services each Sunday and have to sit through the same sermon, word for word, at all of them. The vicar has, however, been heard to express the opinion that as the choir never listen to a single word of the sermon at any service, no great hardship is caused. She is one of those preachers who, from the moment she skips up the pulpit stairs and clamps her all-enveloping gaze on the congregation, can rivet you on the edge of your seat with an irresistible display of sheer dramatics, whose effects remain with you elevatingly until you are at least half-way home. Then you suddenly realize that you haven't the slightest idea what she was talking about.

The choir, being seated in the chancel behind the pulpit, did not come under the spell of the vicar's oratory and were therefore free to do their own thing during the sermon, discussing in hoarse whispers everything from the government to the vicar's new secretary, a recent arrival in the parish who was an accomplished cricketer and was embarrassing everyone by pushing her claim to join the all-male parish cricket team. Then there was the bass who never joined in the gossip but made strange muted growling noises as he practised his part for next Sunday's anthem.

But this Sunday things were different. The vicar was talking about the church music – about the broken-down organ, about the choir, about Teddy and his seventy years' choir service. The choir listened intently, even the bass stopped growling. This sermon was important. You never knew quite which way the vicar would jump. She couldn't read a note of music, and cherished a very simple idea of musical praise which consisted in shrieking everything at the top of your voice and smiling at everyone to show you were enjoying it. And this, of course, didn't necessarily need an organ. The vicar was well on form and perhaps easier to follow than usual. Her gist seemed to be that, far from being a tragedy, the breakdown of the organ should present itself as a golden opportunity for everyone, congregation and choir alike, to join together and sing *from the heart* – one great praising band. 'Togetherness,' proclaimed the vicar, 'wonderful togetherness.'

The man next to me lowered his head into his hands and gazed at his feet. 'It doesn't bear thinking about,' he groaned. He had a point. If there was one thing the congregation at Albert's church never did it was to sing from the heart as one great prais-ing band. They never sang at all. They never had to. They dutifully opened their hymn books at the right place, frowned at the hymn for a few baffled seconds, and then let their interest wander gently where it would while the choir and the organist combined to thunder out the hymn for them in their unique, unrestrained Wagnerian style that could be heard in the next street. No one had ever suggested that the congregation should take part in the musical sections of the service, and the congregation had never contemplated doing so. Tradition is strong and revered in Albert's church.

Serious discussion in the choir vestry followed the service. 'What's she think she's doing, preaching a sermon like that?' fumed Teddy. 'Not in all my seventy years in this choir have I heard such an – an inflammatory suggestion. It's the choir's job to sing. Singing's got nothing to do with the congregation.'

'There's no music in their hymn books, only words,' said the bass. 'They're not supposed to sing.'

'Most of 'em can't read music anyway,' put in the soprano with the shocking pink blouse. 'Well, the people I know in the congregation can't. Mind you, there's some in the *choir* can't read music either.'

'If the vicar gets the congregation joining in the hymns it'll upset the whole balance of our singing,' prophesied the tenor soloist, who always tried to be heard above everyone else even when he wasn't singing a solo. 'You must have *balance*.'

'And that means we must have the organ again,' insisted the bass. 'I thought the sermon would be about getting money for the organ repairs – well, enough of it to get going again. Anti-choir that's what the vicar is – anti-choir.'

The congregation, who had at first shown little interest in the organ fund, suddenly realized after the sermon that the vicar was using the absence of the organ as a ploy to inveigle them into actually having to sing hymns and then be drawn into her outlandish plans for this 'togetherness thing' in the parish. They felt the vicar must be restrained. Tradition must be upheld.

Anti-congregation, that's what the vicar was – anti-congregation. In no time at all, against all expectations, the organ fund had swelled to a size that ensured that at least a good bodging-up job could be done on the instrument.

The other Sunday I visited Albert again. I had intended to take my honorary place in the choir, but owing to the vagaries of the railway people I was late at the church. I found a place in the congregation during the singing of the first hymn, one of my firm favourites, 'Through all the changing scenes of life'. I joined in joyously – and then realized my awful blunder. Surprised, amazed, indignant glares were shafted at me from all quarters. *Singing* in the congregation! I shut up. I stand by tradition!

8

The Old Order Changeth – Back

At the village church where I recently sang in the choir, there hadn't been a new organist for sixty years. And during that time the choir had evolved a completely unique way of singing. This consisted mainly of bawling everything at the tops of their voices and taking breaths whenever they wanted them, in splendid defiance of all the niggling directions of the composer. Everyone had been in the choir for years and years, and no one ever left it, unless they died or were threatened by their wives.

But at last the old organist resigned. His reason for this unbelievable step was vague, but it was something to do with wanting to devote more time to digging up his back garden. Anyway, he had left the choir floundering, and given the vicar a longed-for opportunity to lure into his clutches a new organist who would be willing to introduce all his (the vicar's) favourite modern anthems and tuneless hymn tunes.

The Friday evening choir practice which I attended was far from the usual happy gathering. Three candidates for the post of organist and choir-master were to be auditioned, and were already sitting in a grim row at the back of the church. In the vestry the atmosphere was rather like that of a South American rebellion. The choir had been ordered – actually *ordered* – to be in their places by 8 p.m. sharp. This meant the breaking of a life-time tradition for two or three veteran gentlemen, who always called in at 'The Lamb and Lion' tavern on their way to practice and were never expected to add their weight to the melodious uproar until at least a quarter to nine.

They were having a lively protest meeting in a corner by themselves, while a much larger group were all shouting furiously at each other about the vicar's unreasonable request that, contrary to cus-tom, the choir should be robed during the practice. The vicar had simply said that it would be rather nice if they were robed on this special occasion, but hadn't given the reason why it would be nice. Actually his idea was to hide from the candidates the indescribably filthy jackets of the choirmen – who for the most part came straight to practice from farmyard and garage – and the clothes of some of the teenage girls which were not particularly filthy, but just indescribable.

And as if this wasn't enough, someone had started a malicious rumour that a new organist would expect the choir to read music. This was the last straw. Naturally the choir were outraged. As one man said, this kind of thing was only one step from singing unaccompanied. It was unthinkable.

Suddenly the vicar appeared, clapping his hands, and announced that it was time to start the auditioning. He was a tall, vital young man of great faith, but even he looked a trifle wary as he herded his mutinous mob into the choirstalls.

Quickly taking advantage of the momentary silence as everyone concentrated on glaring down the church at the victims, the vicar smartly introduced the adjudicator, a distinguished, kindly-looking man, who must have now been wondering how on earth he'd got involved in this catastrophe. He could see which way the wind was blowing, and spoke in soothing tones about the great patience he was sure the choir would show during the next hour. Then he called on the first candidate to rehearse us in a hymn and a psalm.

The gentleman came forward to the piano haltingly, took a brief dispirited glance at us, then sat down and played through a hymn without a word. I think his spirit was weighed down with some secret brooding sorrow, because he took no more notice of us, and never even realized that we hadn't started the psalm by the time he'd reached the third verse. Anyway, he was soon dispatched with a bright smile from the vicar, and drifted away, trance-like, into the comforting shadows of the churchyard.

The next candidate now took over. I suppose he could play the piano; but he didn't try. He waved his hands vaguely, and led off the singing of the hymn in an unbelievably flat and quavering alto voice. The choir had never been conducted before, and didn't approve of unaccompanied singing, so they took no notice of him and politely pretended that they were unaware he was singing so flat. He certainly seemed unaware of our lack of enthusiasm. I don't think *he* had any brooding sorrow. I think that, for some reason, he simply didn't want the job. He was quite friendly though. At the end of the psalm he assured us that it had been an unforgettable experience . . .

By this time the choir, despite themselves, were becoming quite interested in the proceedings. They were indeed keen to see what the next turn would be like. And the next turn was priceless!

He was a very young man who obviously knew that only a cathedral choir and organ would be worthy of him. I shall never know why he condescended to honour us with his presence. Perhaps, in a lofty and beautiful way, he had felt some great missionary urge to save us from the darkness of ignorance and debased sentimentality in which the choir had so happily stumbled for the last sixty years. Gently he pointed out to the sopranos that their so-called singing put his teeth on edge, and of the men he tactfully enquired whether they had the faintest idea of the hymn tune which they were supposed to be singing.

In the awed silence which the presence of genius always inspires, he told us that perhaps, if we watched his beat closely and tried *just* the first line of the tune to 'la', he might be able to hammer home our first ever lesson in singing. The choir were so impressed by this that the awed silence continued, despite all his stirring demands that we should open our mouths.

I suppose it's no good casting pearls before swine. The vicar led him gently away.

A month or two later I sang in that choir again. The old organist had got fed up with digging up his back garden and had returned. Enlightenment

9

Smile!

My friend Fog Horn Fred (he used to be headmaster of a senior boys' school not noted for its gentility) is one of those people who can never remember names, however familiar. His absorbing accounts of life in the cosily tucked away Suffolk village to which he retired as soon as possible, and where he now plays the church organ and confuses the choir, are consequently full of colourful references to characters like Mrs-Do-you-know-what-I-think, Mr-You-can't-park-'ere and Her-with-the-cross-eyed-cat.

His latest story, whispered hoarsely to me during the sermon on a recent Sunday when I was a guest in the choir, was well up to standard. It centred on the new vicar and, as usual, the dyed-in-the-wool choir. Now the new vicar, a handsome, middle-aged informally attired (no clerical collar unless the Bishop is about) ever-smiling bachelor, had about him a well established, expertly nurtured public

image of a sympathetic, listening, caring, supportive, thoroughly pleasant person, an image which in
his former parishes had worked most successfully in
ensuring that, however traditionally awkward they
might be, the choir accepted – even eagerly – all
his radical views and plans for their future or demise
without a murmur of dissent, as if they'd thought
of them themselves.

Great was his surprise and sorrow, therefore,
when he took up his duties in Fred's parish and
realized early that, as Fred put it, his image wasn't
going to wash with *this* choir. As soon as he com-
menced his tried and tested procedure of calling a
'vital, consultative, investigative meeting' with the
choir, so that they could democratically agree to all
his exciting plans for altering everything within
reach and thrillingly heaving their Victorian presence into the 21st century, he was confronted with
the choir's feet-thick walls of Jericho. Even before
the meeting had been arranged the vicar had fallen
foul of the choir. He had turned up quite uninvited
at the latest choir practice and, having smiled hugely
at everyone and congratulated them on their very
enjoyable performance at the Sunday services, had
said that they'd give one hundred per cent better,
more professional performances if only they all

smiled as they sang. He had stridden up and down the choirstalls, baring his teeth in a vigorous smile and mouthing as they sang, 'Smile! Smile! You're happy to be here, aren't you? You're *enjoying* your-selves, so *smile*! No, that's only quivering your lips. Come on – light up! Let's have some real praise smiles!' The vicar had then charged off, no doubt, Fred averred, to bludgeon a few more parishioners' sensibilities, and the choir stood around in the vestry in a state of shocked indignation.

The bass whose speciality was to roar AMEN at the end of each hymn (despite the practice having been dropped by the rest of the choir for years and years) was first to recover his voice. 'Grinning while singing,' he mumbled. 'What are we coming to? If we were caught grinning during the service when I was a choirboy we got our choir pay docked fourpence a time. What's the matter with the man?'

'If we all suddenly started grinning all over the place when we were supposed to be singing and trying to keep up with Fred on the organ the con-gregation would think we were up to something,' claimed one of the younger, more attractive sopranos. 'They'd be right annoyed, that's for sure – particularly that lot in the front pews who even complain if one of us sneezes or they can hear us talking during the sermon.'

'Yes, some of them have always enjoyed complaining about us,' agreed the choirman who sang a sort of tenor or whatever was wanted, 'particularly when we sing, but on the whole I think they like us really. After all, they're always very keen to have us around when any of them wants to get married, or christened or buried.'

'True, true,' boomed a contralto lady of regal proportions and presence, known to Fred as 'her-with-the-corrugated-hair'. 'For some reason they're easily upset by us.'

'Yes, the mere sight of us,' confirmed the more attractive soprano. 'Remember the time when I couldn't help smiling at something very rude Fred had said about us breaking down in the anthem. Old churchwarden Frosty Face brought up the collection at the end of the service and thought I was making eyes at him, and went all red and nearly dropped the plate.'

The bass who sang AMEN returned to the fray ponderously. 'When you think about it – you know, sort of really *think* about it – it seems to me singers don't smile when they are singing.' 'They do in opera,' put in the more attractive soprano.

'Only in Gilbert and Sullivan,' admitted the bass, 'and even there you get the contralto soloists – Sullivan made sure of giving the contraltos the real battle-axe parts and you don't see battle-axes smiling. In grand opera nearly *everybody* scowls and rolls their eyes. Grand opera is full of villains and disappointed lovers and there's always someone in dead trouble.'

'Well, we're generally in dead trouble half-way through the "Alleluia Chorus" when we have to do it at Christmas,' reasoned the sort-of-tenor, 'but it wouldn't help if we all started grinning, would it?'

'Well, it would make our new vicar happy,' claimed the corrugated contralto. 'He wouldn't *know* we'd broken down would he! He doesn't know the difference between the "Alleluia Chorus" and "Any Old Iron". So long as we were making some kind of noise and smiling like mad he'd be overjoyed.'

The vicar didn't appear at the next choir practice. Fred reckoned he was concentrating his smiling theory that evening on the bell-ringers, a band of durable-looking gentlemen who habitually appeared arrayed identically in shapeless black suits, dark drooping pullovers, dark drooping moustaches and large boots, and who seemed to spend most of their time, when not ringing, growling to each other spasmodically in the snug of 'The Brown Bear'.

'The vicar's going to have a hard job with that lot,' prophesied the bass who sang AMEN. 'Well, I've never seen any of them actually *smile*,' admitted the sort-of-tenor, 'but they do *laugh* sometimes. It's a low rumbling noise like hot water in a tank, but it doesn't alter their expressions. By looking at them you'd never *know* they were laughing, and the vicar wants our expressions to show we are happy when we are smiling or laughing. There's not much point otherwise.'

'Perhaps the bell-ringers only laugh ironically,' suggested the corrugated contralto. 'And while the choir and the bell-ringers are doing all this smiling, what are the congregation supposed to be doing?' wondered the sort-of-tenor. 'They've all got faces of granite when we are singing the anthem, and they look absolutely furious during the sermon.'

'I think they're supposed to start smiling as soon as they come into church,' said the more attractive soprano. 'There's a semicircle of people all smiling just inside the porch, and you can't get through the doorway without shaking hands with them and smiling – well, you always smile when you shake hands with people, don't you – no matter what you think of them.'

'Thank goodness we haven't got a lot of grinning people blocking up the choir vestry door,' growled the bass who sang AMEN. 'No, there's just Fred demanding that we don't spoil his Sunday lunch by breaking down in the anthem,' agreed the corrugated contralto. 'Much more natural – not so very *contrived*.'

The new vicar is a man of boundless Christian trust and hope. Bleak though the results so far of his smiling campaign, he forged ahead with joyful heart. One morning in the village street he came upon the church treasurer, a truly worthy character, who knew not the ghost of a smile, who was forever warning him about the parlous state of the parish finances and denouncing the whole congregation for their criminal meanness in parish giving. Grimly he acknowledged the vicar. At his side, Oscar his rollicking Boxer dog, looked up at the vicar. Nature had moulded Oscar's wonderful crumpled features into the semblance of a glorious permanent smile. The vicar had never had much time for animals – they had no souls to save. Now, suddenly he began to wonder.

Someone in the parish was smiling!

10

The Take-over

We were reminiscing about the old days, Sam and I, the old days in the parish church choir that he has served for over 60 years. Sam furrowed his brow in silent, searching thought. 'Yes, I can remember exactly when the invasion started – when the front choirstalls started filling with delightful young women instead of fiendish little boys.'

A few years after the end of the Second World War, things were getting comfortably back to normal in the cultural world of the small West Country town where my friend Sam played the organ at the parish church. Among other familiar diversions there was a thriving dramatic society that attempted every kind of theatrical production with exactly the same 'superb, thrilling, scintillating success', according to the local paper, and an operatic society that was doing very well indeed – as long as it didn't actually tackle an opera – with so many ticket-selling members who could get blood out of a stone that the church hall was always packed to the rafters whenever the society put on one of its 'fabulous musical extravaganzas'.

Equally successful was the revived and rapidly-growing writers' circle run by a very popular lady (unanimously re-elected chairwoman every year) who, in return for sumptuous monthly suppers at her listed Georgian home, only required members to listen regularly and appreciatively on Wednesday evenings to her inspired readings, enshrining her latest thoughts on every imaginable topic from the secret life of a grasshopper to the feasibility of introducing triple-decker trams into our major cities.

And the parish church choir, with all their war service members now safely back in their familiar places, were settling down nicely into something of their pre-war (pre- Second, First and Boer War) traditions. Happily, the wartime vicars, two characters who, under the guise of combat conditions, had tried – quite unsuccessfully – to introduce modern hymns, new types of service and all manner of similar subversive ideas, had moved on to upset some other parishes, and the new vicar, far from wanting to turn the clock forward, seemed quite fascinated at finding himself with a genuine nineteenth-century church choir, and was continually putting himself forward to sing the tenor solos in some of the more florid Victorian anthems in which the choir revelled.

The choir was delighted to welcome him. After the vicissitudes and horrors of the war, particularly subversive wartime vicars, they were indeed happy with their lot. There was, it is true, one difference from former days which, as time went on, became only more apparent. It was proving increasingly difficult to recruit new choirboys, and Sam realized that he was having to rely more and more on a growing number of young women for the soprano line.

They weren't the same as boys. He couldn't even *consider* bawling at them during choir practice in the manner familiar to boys; calling them tasteless morons and incredible oafs was simply out of the question. Indeed, being one of the old school who regarded young women – particularly very attractive young women such as now graced the choir-stalls – as those to whom you should be unfailingly polite, not to say charming, in every way, he found himself paying the most outrageous compliments to the new soprano soloist whenever she sang even a single line of the anthem on her own.

Fortunately she was quite used to the numerous

compliments that the undoubted charms of her voice and person regularly brought her, and was neither flattered nor embarrassed, being far more appreciative of compliments paid to her horse, a heavyweight hunter whom she called her baby, and to her family's huge round black tom cat who imposed his will on all the cats for miles around and was known as The Bishop . . .

But the interesting female invasion of the choir in no way distracted from the overall, comfortable, strong feeling that things under the new vicar were set to carry on much in their pre-war manner. His admiration for the choir was boundless, and even though the situation became a bit awkward at times when his enthusiasm led him to turn up at choir practice and drown everybody out with a voice like a tone-deaf foghorn, this was, as Sam said, a small price to pay for having the vicar on the choir's side. One didn't have to go far these days, for instance, to hear heartrending stories of vicars whose main Sunday morning recreation seemed to be that of upsetting the choir by changing all the hymns moments before the service began – or even during the service if the spirit so moved them. And, as Sam said, considering the problems of luring boys into the choir, they really were lucky in having such a

– well – smashing lot of girls on the soprano line. They made the choir quite glamorous – in fact, choral matins was a delight these days. It brightened up Sunday no end.

I could see what he meant. On my first visit to the church after a number of restrictive war years, I could not help noticing the difference inside the vestry as the choir assembled on Sunday morning. The once-familiar mass of choirboys wrestling in and out of the cassock cupboards, scattering sweet papers and peanut shells all over the place, and knocking over piles of hymnals and ancient choir-men, and being reviled in the most lurid terms by Sam, had gone. Only a small group of the remnants of their company, four or five elderly choirboys, now stood in a corner looking rather self-conscious, croaking together with breaking or already-broken voices. Their old stamping ground had changed hands. Now it was a colourful, sparkling place of high girlish chatter and laughter and perfumed air, of little mirrors and pretty combs – a gentle acknowledgement that changing times had touched even Sam's timeless choir.

But, reassuringly, the men of the choir were there as I'd always remembered them, standing in the churchyard just outside the vestry door, all steadily puffing at a collection of villainous-looking pipes and soggy cigars, and producing what we all recognized in those days as a manly atmosphere with rolling banks of manly, suffocating smoke.

One of the smokers, a man who always maintained that as a small child he had been present at the laying of the foundation stone of the church – which would have made him at least one hundred and thirty years old – recognized me immediately and drew me into the fog with a huge horny hand, and there was a warm feeling in recognizing most of the faces I had known before the war.

'It's so good to find you all still here!' I enthused.

'Trouble is, for how long?' rumbled the bass soloist, meditatively blowing a cloud of cigar smoke all over me.

'Well, we're not all that old, are we?' I suggested cheerfully. 'We'll be here for years yet.'

'But we can't last for ever,' he pressed. 'Who's going to sing tenor or bass after us?'

'More tenors and basses, I suppose,' said Horny Hand.

'But where will they come from if we've got no choirboys to train up?'

'These girls – they're the trouble,' grated a tall, stooping man half-hidden in the fog at the back of the group. 'Boys turn into tenors and basses but girls just go on being sopranos.'

'I remember one woman years ago who sang bass,' recalled Horny Hand.

'When was that?' asked a young man who I imagined was a new recruit. 'Was that about the time you were at the foundation-stone laying?'

'She was a very good bass,' insisted Horny Hand. 'Used to announce the trains down at the station.'

The new recruit removed his pipe from his mouth, examined it minutely and tapped it out on the vestry door handle. He said musingly, 'My pal up north is in a church choir that is made up of just three families. All the members of the choir keep marrying each other and so they've always got plenty of boys – and girls – to carry on. They're all brought up to it, yer see. We could have something like that here.'

'I haven't noticed that any of our girls will even go for a drink with you,' retorted the bass soloist. 'There's got to be a quicker way of getting tenors and basses.'

'We'll always have tenors and basses,' prophesied the new recruit. 'They'll come and ask to join the choir. People do. I did.'

'Why should they do that?' asked the half-hidden one.

'Lots of reasons,' assured the ever-optimistic new recruit. 'They might get married here and like the choir and feel they'd like to join.'

'I bet they wouldn't,' averred the bass soloist. 'Not if they'd heard us do "Jesu, joy of man's desiring" at a Saturday wedding,' when the bride's late as usual and half the choir are straining to get away to a match.'

'We don't want any more tenors and basses, anyway,' said Horny Hand. 'We haven't got any spare cassocks and surplices.'

'I don't think you've quite grasped the situation,' said the bass soloist. 'We must think of the future.'

'Sufficient unto the day is the evil thereof,' intoned the half-hidden one.

The vicar pushed his big friendly face round the door. 'Right, chaps, we're ready,' he announced, so we joined the girls and processed into the church.

Matins that Sunday took the form of a special celebration service in honour of the vicar's warden and his wife, who had just completed fifty years of married life. The couple sat close together in the front pew looking apprehensive, backed by four rows of assorted relations who wore everything from smart lounge suits and garden-party dresses to resurrected relics of war-time 'Utility' creations. Scattered throughout the rest of the pews, friends and well-wishers craned their necks amidst the usual congregation, and a party of American tourists, anxious to find out what all the excitement was about, were taking flashlight photographs of everyone within range.

The celebrating couple had chosen all the music for the service, including a very special request, Mendelssohn's 'Hear my prayer', and here the choir ran into a patch of trouble at the very last moment. The famous solo part was to be sung by Georgie, the one remaining choirboy whose voice was not yet in the process of breaking, but he, although being overruled, had shown a marked reluctance to perform, knowing that his mother, who normally didn't attend church ('I used to go to Sunday School, of course, but when you grow up – well, there's so much to do – and Sunday's supposed to be a day of rest, isn't it?'), would make a special effort to be at the service to support her 'clever little lad' with as many of the neighbours as she could round up without using actual physical force. On other occasions when he'd sung a solo during a service his mother and two or three of her more emotional friends had waved to him as the choir had processed into church. Now they were here once again, and once again they waved. And for our solo boy it was once too often. As soon as he reached his stall, his face turned a delicate shade of green and he rushed back into the vestry. 'Emotional upset or cheap chocolate,' pronounced the man next to me. 'That boy eats *tons* of cheap chocolate. He finished off a bag of it in the vestry just now. Never seen anything like it.' He moved away. 'I'd better see what he's up to.'

By the time we'd reached the last verse of the opening hymn, my colleague was back again. 'He'll live,' he reassured. 'He's getting some fresh air outside. But he's still green. He won't be able to do the solo.' He leaned back and whispered the news to Sam at the organ, who said something like 'little cretin', and appeared initially much put out. A few moments later, however, during the prayers which were thundering round the church from the vicar's new microphone (for which he had no need whatsoever), Sam's whole demeanour had changed as he whispered urgently to the new soprano soloist, and beamed at her, and appeared so overcome that it almost seemed he was about to kiss her hand. 'Wonderful, wonderful,' we heard him murmur.

'Oh, splendid – marvellous experience, I'm sure . . .'

'Makes you sick, don't it?' said the man next to me. 'She *can* sing, though. She'll do the solo fine.'

And she certainly did do the solo fine. Even the ranks of Georgie's supporters were reduced to happy tears, even the choirmen all grunted halting congratulatory words to her after the service, certainly the vicar was delighted at such an attractive prospect for increasing the congregation. And Sam became completely entangled and fell over himself, reeling off praises that verged on the poetic.

And the attractive soprano escaped as soon as she politely could to make her way as usual to the stables, where she told her 'baby' that people really were very funny.

Thus, the era of choirboy supremacy ended at my friend Sam's church and the girls took over, and for a while all was well. Eventually two families moved into the area who had a surfeit of small boys. The parents, who were regular churchgoers, thought it would be nice for the boys to be in the choir. The boys all proved to be the usual high-spirited lads or trainee gangsters, depending on your point of view, and all were absolutely unmusical. Nevertheless they looked nice in the front row of the choir in new blue cassocks and crisp white surplices, and were warmly welcomed, particularly by some of the older parishioners who, despite their ready acceptance of the girls, still missed the traditional boys.

Sam considered himself doubly blessed. He loved praising and flattering the girls, and was getting very good at it, but he'd realized of late that he missed more and more letting off steam at the boys. Now he had opportunity for both modes. Tuesday evenings were set aside for boys-only practice and, week after week, his voice roared from the vestry in the good old pre-war way. 'Tasteless morons . . . incredible oafs . . . I've met a few cretins in my time, but *you* lot . . .'

11

All Is Forgiven

My friend, who has been a vicar's warden for twenty-five years, despite the most desperate and crafty efforts to get rid of the job on to someone else, always says that the funny thing about a vicar is that if he wants to become really popular he has to leave the parish. While he is the vicar there, the church is half-empty and everybody says he is the worst man they've ever had to put up with. But if he gets another living and then comes back one Sunday to preach a sermon, the church is packed to the doors, and the whole congregation line up to shake hands with him after the service and remark how much better he is than the new vicar.

My friend in question lives in a London parish and had invited me to swell the choir at Sunday evensong on what was to be a very momentous occasion. The former vicar was to make his first return visit, and big preparations were in hand.

Even had I not been told, I should have known

from the church music list in the local paper that something important was afoot. These lists are most interesting because they give a very good indication of the level of musical culture at each church. They are normally to be found tucked away amidst the In Memoriam notices and the adverts for bedsitters and second-hand gas stoves. The idea is to let you know what hymns you'll be singing if you go to church on the following Sunday, but in the case of musical churches, where they don't like the congregation to sing and upset the beautiful choir, they don't give the hymns at all. Instead they announce a long list of organ voluntaries which the congregation, in their ancient and revered custom, can talk across and walk out on within two minutes of the close of the service.

My friend's church was one of those which plugged the organ voluntaries, but it did also give a list of hymns. For the big day most of the former vicar's favourite hymns were listed. They were quite the opposite from the usual choice of the new vicar who, guided by an astonishingly clever young organist (also new) preferred quiet restful hymns with gentle unaccompanied verses which the people at the back of the church – and they nearly all sat at the back – couldn't hear at all. It was obvious that the new vicar was making great sacrifices to ensure a happy evensong for his predecessor, who was an ex-rugger type and revelled in roaring out Welsh hymn tunes and nineteenth-century mission hymns with tunes like military marches.

But whatever hymns were chosen at my friend's church there was always the possibility of a little snag. You could not rely on singing those advertised. The astoundingly clever young organist was also very temperamental and sometimes, at the last minute, he found that he just *couldn't face* the choir, and it was then that they had to call upon the deputy organist. She was a dainty, flower-like lady of uncertain age, with a name sounding something like Cupid or Stupid, and she could only play about half-a-dozen hymns in a bearable manner. On these occasions, of course, the scope of the choir's efforts was rather cramped.

We were particularly worried about the astoundingly clever young organist as we waited in the vestry a few minutes before the commencement of the big service. The ex-rugger vicar had arrived and was already dispensing crushing handshakes all over the vestry. Every member of the choir had arrived, every server and every sidesman. The congregation crowded the pews like eager supporters at an international match. Only the organist was missing. There was a horrible suspicion, rapidly gaining ground, that the anthem, again one of the former vicar's favourites, was the real trouble. The astoundingly clever young organist had been heard to remark with a shudder that it was a coarse, rowdy thing, unfit for anywhere but the public bar on Boxing Night. It was feared that he would never stand up to it. Only at the last moment, just as they were sending for the flower-like deputy, did he arrive. He looked pale and calm, and a man next to me said reverently, 'He's steeled himself. He's doing a very brave thing.'

The service thundered boisterously on its happy way. The coarse, rowdy anthem went with a tremendous swing. We sang so loudly that the astoundingly clever young organist suddenly couldn't stand it any longer and drowned the lot of us with the full brute force of the organ. The ex-rugger vicar sat erect, exhilarated, and beamed all over his face at the new vicar, who was cupping his face in his hands and discreetly blocking his ears. A much revered ex-mayor in the congregation, who was even more discreetly sorting out some 20 pence coins for the collection, seemed to become paralysed at the mighty sound, and dropped them all down the heating grating, and a small child in the front pew started to stamp and scream in a most extraordinary manner.

But, of course, the main attraction this Sunday was undoubtedly the sermon. The ex-rugger vicar climbed into the pulpit and you could have heard a pin drop after he had performed his well-known, collar-easing, throat-clearing ritual. He gazed fondly at the rows of upturned faces, recognizing especially, no doubt, those belonging to the members who had always so vehemently and consistently disagreed with him on the church council, and had so successfully prevented him from doing anything at all to drag their church out of the middle of the nineteenth century. He said how good it was to see so many old friends all gathered together to welcome him. He recalled with gratitude how they'd all worked so splendidly as a *team* – all pulled *together* and shown such a lively *progressive* interest . . .

By the end of the sermon the whole congregation were bursting with happiness and good humour. The collection did remarkably well, and at the close of the service, the queue to shake hands stretched right up the main aisle. It had been announced that refreshments would be served in the adjoining parish hall, and the choir, who never seemed to join the congregation in anything, not even shaking hands with ex-rugger vicars, got to the counter well in advance of everyone else. Indeed, they had consumed most of the coffee and even the limp oatmeal biscuits, left over from the previous Sunday in a tin without a lid, before the gyrating mass of hand-shakers eventually flowed into the hall.

In the vestry the astoundingly clever young organist was slowly recovering from the effects of the service, and was trying to forget that he had ever been mixed up with the dreadful music which had been so brutally forced upon him. He soothed himself by sorting out some quiet, simple, beautiful music for the next Sunday.

He was feeling that life was almost worth living again when, half-an-hour later, the guest of honour passed back through the vestry, still flanked by as many satellites as could get through the door at the same time. He spotted a lone figure and tackled him immediately. His voice was warm and appreciative.

'May I say how *very* much I enjoyed your playing tonight!' He took the astoundingly clever young organist's hand in his paralysing grip. 'So many young church organists these days seem afraid of a good singable tune – seem scared of letting out the organ in a good burst of sound. No *spirit* in them! No *joy!*' He turned to the satellites. 'Mark my words, this young man will go a long way. He's got the right *idea*. No worry about the choir while *he's* in charge.' He slapped the young man on the shoulder. 'Keep up the good work! I shall remember that anthem for a *long* time. Splendid!'

Later that evening I saw the astoundingly clever young organist making his way home. He walked slowly, unseeingly, like a broken man.

connected with Handel's 'Messiah'. The event is always advertised by a large poster, completely covering the notice board, which is the work of the organist's granddaughter, who loves horses but not the children who ride them, and is a very successful illustrator of children's books. It is bordered by fat cherubs, bulbous Father Christmases, and horses' heads, and proclaims: 'Highlights from "Messiah" – come and join in. Bring your own music. Thanksgiving collection for charity.'

How and why the event originated is lost in history. The choir say they've always done it. The parish is full of such traditions and all are unassailable, as a recent new vicar was forced to realize to his sorrow. He had suggested to the church council that, in the cause of inter-parish fellowship and co-operation, after the next 'Messiah highlights' the event should be replaced by a concert by the Ladies' Madrigal Society from a neighbouring village.

At that year's 'Highlights' performance more than twice the usual number of parishioners – with their music – turned up to take part, and one or two who couldn't lay their hands on a 'Messiah' were seen with 'Elijah' or 'The Damnation of Faust' under their arms. The message was clear. The new vicar capitulated in the face of tradition, even to the extent of enthusing over the revered annual custom of the three-hour peal of bells (the bell tower is a few feet from the vicar's bedroom window) from nine p.m. until midnight in celebration of the organist's birthday.

Despite this joyous prolonged tribute, however, no one really seems to know how old the organist is. No one in the choir can remember when he wasn't there, and he presents a very well-preserved appearance. In fact he is so well-preserved that he doesn't seem to have grown any older for years. Like his organist's gown, his Sunday buttonhole, his car and his choice of music, he never changes, and all this makes his choir – one of the last all-male strongholds in the Church of England, it would seem – a very comfortable and pleasant organization to belong to, particularly if you can't read a note of music, don't understand musical terms and find it difficult to spot the place in the anthem where you are supposed to come in. He explains things in everyday language that even the most unmusical choir member can understand. When, for instance, the tenors get to sound too much like an enraged football crowd in a passage of music marked *tranquillo*, he remarks mildly, 'Now we don't want it a yard wide, do we? Put the brakes on a bit,' and if the treble soloist is missing the point entirely, he recommends gently, 'It'll help, lad, if you turn to the right page – and then put some beef into it.'

And now, once again, Christmas was approaching, and yet another 'Messiah highlights' was in the offing. I had come to stay with cousin Henry for the occasion. We had had our final rehearsal and were looking forward gleefully to the performance in two days' time (the most gleeful anticipation of the choir, as usual, being the result achieved when the congregation joined them in rendering the Alleluia Chorus).

And then the blow fell.

Some kind of virus had hit the village with lightning speed and, although most of the men of the choir appeared to have evaded it, every one of the boys was reported out of action.

On that Saturday evening the organist called the men to an emergency meeting in the vestry, and it soon became very clear that the performance would have to be cancelled – an unthinkable calamity. Even Ancient Abel couldn't help in this situation, although Abel is unique. It is not possible to pinpoint what kind of voice he has. Strictly speaking his is not a conventional voicebox, it's more of a super-adaptable piece of apparatus capable of producing almost any kind of sound imaginable. And this makes him very useful when the choir is short of an alto, tenor or bass. I've heard him produce the most ear-splitting falsetto with the utmost ease, and his huge Chaliapin-like bass voice is just as devastating, while his sobbing Italian tenor is one of the most moving sounds I know. In fact, my cousin Henry says it moves people away as far as possible in no time at all. But even Abel couldn't imitate a dozen trebles.

It was at this last bewildering moment that the vicar bounced into the vestry, full of enthusiasm and kind thoughts. Everything was going to be all right. We needn't worry. He had been on the phone to the Ladies' Madrigal Society – the one, we would remember, that he had suggested should give a Christmas concert as an alternative to the 'Messiah highlights'. All the ladies were very willing to help the choir out of its difficulties. It would be such a splendid exercise in inter-parish fellowship and co-operation.

Long after the vicar had gone, the choirmen sat in a stunned, silent circle.

Presently it started to get dark and we could hardly see the dismay on each other's faces. Abel got up slowly, still in a state of shock, and automatically switched on the vestry light, which promptly fused. Trance-like, he moved to a surviving gas lamp over the piano. Without a glance at it, he lit it with his pipe lighter. It whistled and flickered. He came back to the rest of the group, who were all gazing unseeingly at the floor. 'It's come to this,' grated Abel. 'It's actually come to this. Women in our choir!'

'Never been known,' fumed our bass soloist.

'Women!' echoed Henry, hollowly.

'Handel had women in the choir at the first performance of "Messiah" in Dublin,' I offered, meaning to be helpful. Immediately I realized my awful bloomer.

'This is not Dublin, and Handel's got nothing to do with our "Messiah" performance,' reprimanded the organist. 'Things have got a bit different since his day – they have here anyway. If Handel heard our choir, he wouldn't want women butting in. He'd realize . . .'

We didn't hear what Handel would realize about our choir, for at that point the vicar, still all helpful smiles, put his head round the door. 'I've just arranged for a coach to pick up the ladies tomorrow evening,' he announced. 'Isn't it splendid?' He was too elated to notice the state of the assembled company. He turned to leave and, noting the lighted gas lamp, gave an amazed chuckle. 'Good heavens, I didn't know that thing still worked. It takes me back to the church where I was a choirboy. We still had gas lighting there. It's funny how the church hangs on to old-fashioned ideas long after everyone else has gone ahead.' He still didn't notice the state of the assembled company.

When I arrived at the church on the evening of the performance, the Ladies' Madrigal Society, all dressed in their black 'concert' dresses and carrying their 'Messiah' copies and large bulging handbags, were grouped at one end of the vestry, and our choirmen were lurking at the other end. In the wide space between them the vicar ambled up and down, rather aimlessly I thought, smiling vaguely as he threw out cheerful remarks to both sides, trying to bring them together. He wasn't being very success-ful, although one very attractive girl from the ladies' camp did brave our countenances and venture across the divide to say how very much she admired our red cassocks, which looked so much better than those used by the choir of her church, which were black, almost turning green. She addressed herself particularly to one of our younger and more impressionable tenors, who in return started enthusing about her dress until he suddenly became aware of the looks of his colleagues and promptly backed in confusion into the cassock cupboard.

And so, for the first time ever, ladies sang in the choir in my cousin Henry's church. As usual the place was packed and, despite the untraditional make-up of the choir, the congregation at least – in the words of the rather superior vicar's warden – 'thoroughly enjoyed themselves murdering Handel'.

In the vestry afterwards the vicar congratulated the choir on leading another unusual, indeed refreshingly different, performance of 'Messiah', and added a very special word of thanks to the Ladies' Madrigal Society who, after all, had saved the day and ensured that a well-loved local tradition was not broken. He then invited us all to partake of a little light refreshment before we bade farewell to our guests, so we all crowded round a small trestle table, behind which were two very large cross-looking ladies, who said that we had finished much earlier than we did last year and the water for the tea and coffee had not yet boiled, so we'd have to wait – and if we kept on pushing against the table, the whole thing would collapse and we'd get nothing. So we all backed off and talked together and nibbled mince pies, which tasted strongly of dripping, until the tea and coffee materialized and we were all able to wash away the dripping taste and see the ladies off in their coach.

When they had gone, the choirmen returned to the church to 'clear up the choirstalls', which seemed to consist of sitting around in the vestry and watching Abel trying to light his pipe – something I had never seen him accomplish. At the end of a long quiet period, during which Abel made three or four dozen attempts to achieve his aim until his lighter finally gave up, obliging him to use a candle taper, which proved equally ineffective, the young tenor in the admired red cassock said, 'She's right, you know – these *are* smart cassocks – very smart.'

To my surprise he met with no rebuff. The organist said slowly, 'Apparently the organ in the church where this madrigal lot come from is very fine – very big. The only trouble is they haven't got a proper choir – no men. They reckon that if we did our "Messiah highlights" there next year, as well as here, it would be a roaring success. The church is bigger than ours and they said we'd fill it to the doors.'

'One of them told me that it was absolutely thrilling singing with such a professional male-voice choir as ours,' said our alto, who was still nibbling cautiously at one of the dripping mince pies. 'It was the blonde one with the big red bow.'

'Big red bow where?' asked Henry.

'On her head,' said the alto.

'Ah, it was the other one who spoke to me, then,' clarified Henry, 'the one with the bow round her neck. She said her brother was something to do with the recording business and she could get him interested, if we sang in their church next year.'

'What about our boys? They must come too,' put in the bass soloist.

'Of course,' confirmed the organist, 'us, the boys and the madrigal crowd – and their great big organ. The lot! Lovely!'

'Nice crowd, really,' mused Henry. 'Sing well – appreciate us.'

Abel at last gave up his attempts to light his pipe. He tapped it out all over the heating stove. 'Women!' he growled.

Oft in Danger, Oft in Woe

I have never been able to understand maps. Once I was supposed to be cycling to a Stately Home and ended up, worn out, at the biggest brewery I had ever seen. Another time, when I thought I was heading for a horse show on a large East Anglian farm, I found myself on quite another farm, helping a stone-deaf farmer to lift an acre of mangold-wurzels.

Even very simple maps fox me. A friend once produced a map which was so simple that most of the places I wished to visit weren't on it at all, and I still lost my way and had to ask a policeman. And I didn't get much further even then. The policeman was brand-new to the area, but was most kind and helpful, and quickly came up with an attractive little road map, to which he said I was most welcome with his compliments . . .

So when, a few months ago, a friend in Somerset sent me an invitation to visit him, and enclosed a map for my guidance, I experienced the thrilling mysterious feeling which all those who took part in the early voyages of discovery must have known – the feeling of wondering where on earth you are going to end up.

That weekend I packed a bag and got as far as Paddington Station quite easily, because I know my way there without recourse to a map. Soon I was hurtling westward behind a monstrous bad-tempered diesel locomotive that kept jerking the train violently from end to end, and emitting belligerent, toneless whistles. And it was when a more than usually vicious jerk had thrown me across the compartment that I discovered, to my huge delight, that the elderly clergyman sitting opposite was a fellow railway enthusiast. As I picked myself up from the crumpled remains of *The Daily Telegraph* on his knees, he said that he was sure I realized that we were in the throes of an age of progress, and must naturally expect to be hurled about railway carriages, because diesel engines were definitely more modern than steam engines and gave a lot more work to people by regularly and unfailingly breaking down. He reckoned that with a bit of luck we should be able to hang on to our seats more successfully after we'd passed Ealing Broadway. He said he made the journey often, and the engine always seemed to quieten down after Ealing Broadway. It was almost as if it didn't *like* Ealing Broadway . . .

My clerical friend and I were the only passengers in the compartment, which I had specially chosen because it was a non-smoker, so, after he had settled himself comfortably in his corner, pulled out a pipe, and filled the place with smoke, he started to tell me about himself. I was delighted to learn that he was the vicar of the neighbouring village to where I was bound. He explained that we left the train at the same station and, since the local branch line was long since closed, we should have to take a bus for the rest of the journey. I gathered that the bus was the very latest in luxury transport, and a great improvement on the late veteran train. And you only had to wait half-an-hour for it, or, if you were of an impatient nature, you could go to the other end of the village where you stood a good chance of catching another bus, provided that you were capable of running at thirty miles per hour and the bus was late leaving.

Meanwhile, we got along splendidly. Apart from his enthusiasm for railways, it transpired that the vicar was a man after my own heart in more ways than one, for he was an ardent admirer of brewery horses, steamrollers and *Hymns A & M*. He also liked collecting antiques, and in his spare time assisted his sister, who ran an antique shop next door to his church. Apparently it was a very exclusive antique shop which offered the most outrageous knick-knacks at the most outrageous prices to people who couldn't stand the sight of them but were determined to be in fashion. The vicar said his sister was a very religious woman, well known at all the local church jumble sales, where she was always allowed in before the general public. In return for this favour, she graciously handed over a ten pound note, and expertly pillaged the most atrocious pieces from the white elephant stall. She then conveyed them lovingly to her shop where, in the dignified and cultured atmosphere behind the Georgian bow-window, they immediately increased their value an hundredfold.

When we eventually arrived at our station, I had almost forgotten the friend whom I was supposed to be visiting, but, when I recalled him, the vicar insisted that I should pop along to see his church first and then he would drive me over to my friend's house later in the evening.

In the station yard the vicar was immediately greeted by his churchwarden, who was the local builder, and had just collected some material from the goods yard. He wouldn't hear of us waiting half-an-hour for the station bus, or running at thirty miles per hour to the end of the village to waylay the other bus. He ushered us into the cab of his lorry and guaranteed to deliver us to the church in no time at all. He said that he only had a few deliveries to make on the way.

I certainly appreciated his Christian action. We made a detour of twenty-five miles, delivered four fireplaces, a thirty-gallon tank, and half a ton of cement, and almost succeeded in running over the Methodist minister's housekeeper and bull-terrier. And we arrived at the church just an hour and a half after the bus.

As dusk had now fallen, the vicar regretted that I wouldn't be able to appreciate the stained-glass windows – the church had some fine 'dim religious light' efforts – but he was sure I would be interested in the pulpit, which Cromwell's soldiers had ruined by decapitating its cherubs, and the choirstalls, which the choir had ruined by carving their names all over them.

As we walked up the churchyard path, a mob of boys charged reverently past us in the opposite direction.

'Choir practice just over,' the vicar explained. 'A really enthusiastic lot we've got here. Full of life!' At that moment another choirboy, who seemed even more full of life, cannoned into the vicar and vanished discreetly. The vicar steadied himself against a tombstone and gazed after him proudly.

'There he goes,' he said, 'the worst hooligan in the choir – got a voice like an angel.' He became confidential. 'Actually, the organist of your friend's church is always trying to lure him into his choir, but the lad is *absolutely* loyal. Absolutely! He seems to love our church. There isn't a member of the congregation he hasn't upset. Yes, I think we can safely say we are stuck with him for good.'

My friend couldn't stop laughing. 'But I don't understand,' he guffawed, after the vicar had delivered me to him at midnight. 'What's all this about diesel engines and lorries and antique shops and choirboys? You only had to follow my map – direct route from London by coach. Get off at "The Lion" and take the first on the right.'

'I never could read maps,' I said.

door during the singing of the hymn before his sermon.

He had often suggested to his warden, in a roundabout way of course, that perhaps a note could be kept of the alleged offenders, but the warden had been warden to a long line of vicars of all kinds, from the autocratic to the 'all jolly chums together' variety, and regarded them all merely as ships that passed in the night, so he gave nothing away and deftly turned the conversation on to items like the reception arrangements for the Mayor and Corporation at the annual civic service, or the leaking chancel roof over the back row of the choir.

In fact, the leaking roof over the back row of the choir had been a problem for quite a number of years. No one seemed able to repair the area permanently. A succession of members of the congregation – a schoolteacher, a bus driver, an operatic tenor and a library assistant – doing a voluntary stewardship job for the church on their days off, had clambered on to the roof with slates and coils of stuff and large tins of sticky liquid, and all had been well for a month or two, but then the whole thing started again. By this time the vicar dreaded to hear of anything remotely connected with the leaking roof over the back row of the choir – indeed, he dreaded to hear of anything to do with the choir at all. Apart from the fact that they steadfastly refused to sing his kind of music and, as a body on the church council, always blocked his dearest wishes to level off the graveyard and stand all the headstones in a nice, neat, tidy line along the path to the church door, and to introduce a lily pond and a picnic area, he simply didn't trust the choir. For a long time he had had his suspicions that here too quite a number of them regularly evaded his sermons although, unlike the congregation backsliders, they didn't actually leave the building but simply retired to the vestry to read their Sunday papers, and then returned to their places for the final hymn.

The trouble was that during the sermon the vicar couldn't see the choir from the pulpit, and this enhanced his suspicions of them because he had always believed that keeping a constant eye on the choir was a very important part of conducting a trouble-free service. A contributing difficulty for the vicar, particularly at evensong on dark winter evenings, was the custom of putting out most of the lights for the sermon except for a spotlight over the pulpit. All he could see from his bright, exalted position were pale blurs of what he took to be upturned interested faces but which he sometimes realized to his chagrin could equally be the tops of heads as they drooped in sleep. He had given the matter much thought and had tried a number of ruses in order to hold the attention of the pale blurs. Once, he started his sermon by singing a verse of a comic song instead of quoting a text, and another time he opened by announcing, 'It's simply bucketing down outside, so you'll all be far better off in here listening to me' – and smiled to show he was only joking, but on both occasions he had the distinct impression that some of the pale blurs had then disappeared altogether.

In his early days in the parish he had, of course, more than once suggested the obvious – that the lights should be left on during the sermon, but here he had met what he finally realized was the original unmovable object. Within living memory the lights had *always* been put out for the sermon. The current man whose job it was to switch them off had done so for over thirty years, except when he had been on holiday. Then the operation had been faithfully carried out by his friend, who was universally regarded as his natural successor and who, for the last twenty-five years, had firmly closed the prison-like West door of the church immediately the ser-

A man standing next to me confided that it was always particularly awkward for him when we all had to sit together on one side while they were mending the roof because he found the atmosphere very claustrophobic. He told me this very loudly (he was a very loud bass), and a large contralto lady floating at my other side said she *never* felt claustrophobic in crowds. In fact she adored crowds, and always loved going to football matches and winter sales. My claustrophobic colleague seemed a mite put out by this, and I think he would have said more had not the vicar at that moment sped into the vestry, bellowed, 'Good morning!' and the vestry prayer all in one breath, and hustled us before him into the church. We all made quickly for the limited accommodation in the mainly unobstructed choirstalls on one side, but had to mill around in a rather undignified manner while a soprano lady with a minute lace handkerchief attempted to remove some outlying plaster dust from the large space she had grabbed. Eventually I found myself sitting at the end of a stall balancing on two retired hassocks that were bursting at the seams and had been hastily brought from the vestry, where they normally supported a three-legged cupboard full of music, forgotten umbrellas and empty wine bottles.

However, I was suddenly aware of the presence, threatening to envelop me, of the contralto lady who adored crowds. Equally, she did not adore people like me, who drifted into the choir at odd times and took up valuable space. With a smart tap or two on the back of my neck from her outsized handbag, she indicated that she had no seat, and not wanting to offer her such a basic one as mine I slipped back into the vestry in the slender hope of finding an overlooked chair or some less disreputable hassocks. I was unsuccessful, of course, and returned to find the lady firmly in possession of my hassocks so, with no other choice, I made myself scarce, sitting on a most uncomfortable eighteenth-century tomb, which had been cavalierly blocked off by the Victorian choirstalls, where I stayed throughout the service. I don't know what the sermon was about because I couldn't hear it from my position, but I did find some fascinating reading in the epitaph which crammed itself all over the front and half-way down one side of the tomb.

Apparently the occupant had been an undeniably perfect human being – a peerless paragon of a fellow – pious, generous and loyal, blameless, gentle and charitable, kind to his wife, children, servants and passing vagrants, and always full of pity for those the vicar sorting some papers in his stall in the chancel. I asked him how things were going and received a most enthusiastic reply. He pointed to various parts of the church. 'How about that!' he said. 'Brand-new lighting system throughout. Only been in a month.' He obviously noted my look of surprise. 'Yes, cost quite a packet,' he beamed. 'But things have been happening around here, I can tell you. We've got a new treasurer – young, very keen type – into everything. Went through the books with a fine toothcomb. Unearthed some sort of church fund going back to the eighteenth century. Seems to have been forgotten and hidden for years.' He pointed to my late uncomfortable seat, the paragon's tomb. 'Matter of fact, it appears *he* started it for providing church candles. Anyway, we used it for the lights and they're the very latest. You can dim them, like theatre and cinema lights. Our man who sees to the lights –'

'Puts them out for the sermon,' I dared.

He grinned. 'Well, he's absolutely *fascinated* and, of course, we only *dim* them for the sermon now. I can see everyone quite clearly.' His eyes twinkled. 'So much *nicer*, I find.'

'And what about the leak over the choirstalls?' I ventured.

15

The Carved Work Thereof

It is always a pleasant experience to visit my Uncle Bert's village church. It's not Uncle Bert's church really, of course, but it's named after such an obscure saint that I can never remember his name or what he did, whereas I know Uncle Bert and what he does very well. He's always getting his name in the papers at the foot of explosive letters of objection on every subject you can think of, and some you would never have thought of. He writes regularly to bishops and cabinet minister and, as a representative of the choir on the parochial church council, enlivens the meetings of that otherwise somnolent body no end with fiery challenges and unanswerable questions. When the vicar wants something to be done in the church and not just argued about at the PCC he sends for Uncle Bert, and everything works out wonderfully. But recently the vicar sent for Uncle Bert once too often.

The choirstalls at Uncle Bert's church were what

the vicar described as 'nearing the end of their useful life'. If he was referring to their ability to accommodate members of the choir and their music, he was wrong. They had solidly done their job for over a hundred and fifty years, and were sturdily capable of continuing to do so, but if the vicar was referring to their capacity to accept any more choirboys' names carved into them, he was right. There was now hardly a square inch of uncarved surface remaining. Anyway, the vicar, a young man who tended to regard church choirs as 'groups', and preferred seeing them perched on chrome and plastic stools backed by a guitar and drums rather than in choirstalls accompanied by the organ, felt he now had a good case for getting rid of the stalls and taking a step towards the chrome and plastic stools.

The fatal mistake he made was to ask Uncle Bert to arrange things so that the parishioners would be in favour of the removal of the stalls and everything would proceed smoothly. Normally Uncle Bert could be relied on to employ his undoubted expertise in favour of the vicar, but this time the vicar's suggestion horrified him. Weren't there the names of generations of his family carved on those stalls? Indeed, hadn't every member of the present choir at least one ancestor whose name appeared among the scores immortalized on the stalls? Good heavens! This was history. At places like Eton College they were proud of all those names carved all over the place. The parish was proud of its church choir. It revered the mementoes of its past choir members. Uncle Bert would certainly have nothing to do with the removal of the stalls. Indeed, Uncle Bert would, as usual, be positive. He would oppose their removal – he would organize the opposition.

During the following weeks, he wrote long impassioned letters to the local paper and the county magazine, extolling the 'priceless relics' that the village church contained in the shape of its 'unique choirstalls where generations of local families have sung and left their names engraved for all time.'

A young press reporter, who had himself sung in the choir as a boy soprano but had never realized that week after week he was lolling about in a priceless relic, was despatched to the vicar to get his views. The vicar took him into church, confronted him with the stalls, and asked him to 'just take an honest look at the awfulness of it all'. The young reporter looked and found his own name – scratched on the back of his seat, he remembered, with an instrument attached to his pocket knife designed for taking stones out of horses' hooves.

'Carving! I ask you!' appealed the vicar tensely. 'Just scratched, scrawled, illiterate graffiti. You will, I'm sure, appreciate my anxiety to have these unworthy things removed.' The young reporter nodded noncommittally and allowed himself to be conducted around the church to be shown some of the finer features he had never noticed as a boy – the medieval stained glass, the eighteenth-century font, the rare brass they had discovered when removing a piece of moth-eaten Victorian stair carpet from the vicar's stall, the memorial to a famous landscape painter whose marble likeness now peered gloomily from behind the packing-case-like erection housing the blowing apparatus of the organ. The vicar concluded the tour by demonstrating the new apricot-coloured concealed lighting of which he was very proud, having installed it himself. How, he asked, could those awful choirstalls be allowed any longer to exist amongst all this beauty and artistry . . . ? As the young reporter departed, the vicar felt sure he had created the right impression and that he could depend on a most sympathetic supportive article in the local paper.

I learned the story so far from Uncle Bert when

I arrived for a week's holiday with him, just as the choirstalls squall was developing into a fully-fledged storm.

News of the controversy had seeped into some sections of the national press, and Uncle Bert reckoned that lately there'd hardly been a moment during the day when some stranger wasn't standing staring at the choirstalls. Even regular members of the congregation came into the church at odd times during the week, to look at the choirstalls that they'd seen every Sunday for years and years. Visitors from far and near took photographs from all angles, not a few sprawling on the chancel floor eating sandwiches and making drawings and copious notes. The choir, who liked their choirstalls and wanted to retain them much more than they did their vicar, had seized on the opportunity for publicity and arranged for two of their most attractive sopranos to be seen lovingly polishing the stalls at frequent intervals during the weekends when visitors were most numerous. Uncle Bert said that to his knowledge the stalls hadn't been polished for at least twenty years, so the girls found plenty of genuine work to do and the whole performance was most convincing, right down to the hoovering of the odd bits of carpet that the choir members had introduced over the years to make the seating more comfortable. Total strangers came and saw and smiled encouragingly at the girls, and went away seething with anger at the insensitiveness of the vicar.

Soon after my arrival on Sunday afternoon, Uncle Bert said we should go along to the church to see what was happening, and we found what was now the usual crowd of sightseers milling around the choirstalls, with the vicar vainly attempting to draw them off to view the other church features. No one seemed the slightest bit interested in stained glass or fonts or even the apricot concealed lighting. They'd come to see the choirstalls, and that was that. A small group of visitors huddled on their haunches as a large, round, bass choir gentleman on his knees pointed out a list of four names scratched deeply at the foot of one stall. 'My grandfather and three great-uncles,' he announced proudly, 'all boys in the choir a hundred years ago. See what they've written,' – and he pointed even lower to a single word, 'Champions' – 'How about that?' he beamed.

'Champion whats?' asked a little man, squinting through a reading glass two inches from the wording.

'My grandfather and great-uncles were champions at everything,' answered the bass, in a tone of finality. 'And look at this.' He pointed further along the panel to a name that began with 'Charlie' but faded out into some indecipherable hieroglyphics and ended up as a large hole bored right through the wood. 'A marvellous bloke, was Charlie,' recollected the bass. 'In the choir for forty-six years. Couldn't sing a note. Completely tone-deaf but he organized the finest choir outings we've ever had, and when he was captain of the choir football team we only lost two matches in four seasons. There aren't many choirmen around like Charlie these days.'

At this point the choir's oldest member, a man who had been the most popular lead in the local dramatic society before the Second World War, made an impressive entrance and started telling the crowd heart-warming tales of choir members commemorated on the stalls, many of whom he had known and still sadly missed – 'Fine, wonderful colleagues and friends, the like of whom I don't expect to meet again.' Everyone gathered round and shook his hand amidst a frenzy of flashlight photography, during which the vicar quietly slipped away with a deeply thoughtful expression on his face.

Uncle Bert reckoned that things were going well. 'Let's go home and have some tea,' he said, 'and then come back and sing in the choir at evensong. It's going to be good tonight.'

Two hours later we were back in church, crammed into the choirstalls, which reeked of polish and by this time were very slippery. The vicar gave the choirstalls (or it may have been the choir) an unfathomable look, and announced the opening hymn to a congregation rather larger than the usual dozen and a half sterling characters who regularly managed to resist the lure of television for an hour on Sunday evenings. The pews were overflowing, and a crowd of people, including a badly-behaved infant and a large well-behaved dog, were marshalled at the back of the church.

Never having had to cater for such a large congregation, the supply of hymn books had given out and people were looking three over a book, although after singing the first verse of a rather unfamiliar hymn most gave up trying to read the second verse and started gazing vaguely all over the place or taking a more particular interest in a man with a press camera, who kept on crawling up and down the side aisle and appearing round the pillars. I had a distinct impression that Uncle Bert's efforts on behalf of the choirstalls were reaching a climax.

As usual, the singing of the psalm and canticles was left to the choir and, while we were singing the Nunc Dimittis, the small badly-behaved infant scrabbled up to the choir screen and glared at us, waving a plastic gun in a most menacing way until the large well-behaved dog appeared and nudged him back to his place.

And so we reached the sermon. The vicar, in his most chatty manner, said how good it was to be able to welcome so many visitors to this historic church. Being rather in the backwoods it had, perhaps, been overlooked in the past but now he was absolutely delighted to report that just before the start of this evening's service he had been invited by the editor of a most prestigious national magazine to contribute a major article on the church and its treasures and traditions – treasures and traditions that must be preserved and guarded, for while ever looking ahead the Church must not forget its past from which it was moulded ... the vicar chatted on and on. He finished strongly. 'But whatever a church possesses, let us always remember that it is its members – people – that really matter – the faithful throughout the ages. On seeing our historic, indeed unique, choirstalls – an

16

Coach Parties Welcome

An unusual feature of the squat little round-towered Suffolk church was its extremely wide middle aisle. And the vicar was a 'middle aisle' man, that is, he never read the lessons from the lectern nor preached from the pulpit. Always he stood in the middle aisle, an ascetic, saintly-looking figure, and presented all he read and said in the sort of matey manner normally experienced in the village pub. He was a 'middle aisle' man in everything. He never took sides among the various warring factions in the parish, although he was always ready to be enthusiastic about the ideas of one faction provided no one from another faction was within earshot.

The only organization in the parish over which he had no need to be diplomatic was the church choir. Everybody agreed about the choir. The same members had been in the choir for countless years. They always sang the same kind of music in the same way, few could read music and they never learned anything new at all. They were quite dreadful – and were held in the highest esteem and regarded with the greatest affection by the whole parish.

They were an institution, a tradition. The vicar knew that he could always rely on the choir being in their places for morning and evening service every Sunday, whatever the state of the weather or the world. Indeed, he sometimes thought nostalgically of the pleasant unscheduled Sunday evenings off he had enjoyed in a former parish, when inclement weather or an unmissable television programme had persuaded choir and congregation to give evensong a miss. Here he had no such expectations. Even if the congregation proved fickle, the choir didn't. They were always there in force and expected nothing less than a full choral evensong and sermon. They'd always been *used* to a full choral evensong and sermon.

I had known Mr Humphreys, the organist and choirmaster, for over twenty-five years (he was always referred to as Mr Humphreys, and no one ever seemed to be sure of his Christian name), and had a standing invitation to sing in the choir whenever I found myself in the vicinity. And one streaming wet and blustery cold Sunday evening in

November, fate, in the guise of the non-appearance of a local train that had slithered off the rails and ploughed into a field of sugar beet, found me stranded near the village, so I splashed along to evensong with a few minutes to spare. The pews of the little church were empty, and the one bell-ringer of the usual team who had turned up was doing his best tolling the tenor bell in fine funereal style. He grinned at me broadly and invited me to hang my sodden raincoat over the font. At a little distance from him, parked at the back of a deep, dim, dusty ceremonial chair, was his grandson, a knowing-looking rotund infant wearing a shiny yellow mac and a red-and-white woolly hat shaped like a basin. The rotund one bawled, 'I jumped in a big puddle!'

'I'll give him puddle,' said grandfather.

'I splashed mud all over him,' continued the rotund one.

'He really *likes* coming to church,' enthused grandfather. 'Never misses. It's very encouraging. When we get him into the bell-ringing he'll be a *regular* – not like some of the types we've got in the tower these days. Where are they tonight, for instance?'

'In the pub!' shouted the rotund one.

'Course, the congregation are no better,' mused

grandfather. 'A drop of rain, and where are they?'

'In the pub!' shrieked the rotund one.

'Anyway, *they're* all here,' assured grandfather proudly, nodding towards the choir vestry. 'Every one of the choir here as usual. They're doing the Alleluiah Chorus tonight. Pity there'll be no one to hear 'em. They should be singing to a big congregation.'

'In the pub!' bellowed the rotund one.

There were about a dozen soaking wet choir members in the vestry, all shaking macs and umbrellas at each other, and recounting their personal misfortunes experienced while endeavouring to get to evensong. There was the cosseted car that wouldn't start, the bus that never appeared, the farm lorry that thought it funny to miss you by inches in a narrow lane and drench you with mud, the water-logged 'short cut' blocked by a broken-down tractor, the automatic umbrella that flew off into the night when you pressed the button, and the cat that shot out in front of your bike and caused you to end up in a ditch full of nettles and discarded milk crates.

Nevertheless, everyone had arrived on time and, having squelched around me shaking hands in their usual most friendly welcome, we sorted ourselves into line for what was normally a dignified procession into the chancel – although on this occasion the rubber boots covered in mud with which most members were sensibly equipped would make the dignity a bit difficult.

We were on the point of moving off when the outer vestry door burst open and a huddled figure, enveloped in a shapeless hooded anorak and carrying a clipboard of rain-pulped papers, staggered in and gurgled, 'Excuse me, can we look round the church?' The hood was thrown back and we saw the face of a very worried young man. 'I've got a coach load of people outside,' he revealed. 'We're a church group from London on a tour of some East Anglian churches. We seem to have lost our way completely since the last church. We've been dodging about for miles and miles – what with this weather and Suffolk being so flat, everything looks the same.' He sneezed. 'This church doesn't seem to be on our itinerary but we thought we could look around now we're here.'

The vicar, whose saintly face wore a calm serene expression – probably because he was the only one in the place who hadn't been soaked to the skin getting to church, the vicarage being directly connected to the vestry – explained gently that evensong was about to begin, and the young man said oh dear, yes, of course, he'd forgotten all about evensong. In their church in London they didn't have evensong any more. They had a really jolly family service in the morning, and in the evening people dropped in at the church's community centre for games and drama and exciting discussions. The vicar said that his church didn't run to any of those refinements so it was evensong or nothing. The coach party would be very welcome, and his wife could rustle up a cup of tea or something after the service.

The coach party quickly decided that in the circumstances evensong *was* better than nothing, and when the service began we had a congregation that filled half the church, which, as the choirman next to me remarked, wasn't bad for such a dirty night when we'd only expected the bell-ringer and that little fiend of his to be in the congregation.

True, the imported faithful looked a bit bewildered when the *Book of Common Prayer* was circulated, and rather apprehensive when volumes of an early edition of *Hymns A & M* were provided and the organ began to play, but they were very polite and tried to join in. It was hard to guess what they thought of our rendering of Handel's Alleluiah

Chorus – it was hard to guess what Handel would have thought – but they all sat very still with fixed expressions as if they were afraid of upsetting something and, at the end, someone started to clap. Then, when we reached the sermon, and the vicar, despite his saintly unbattered-by-the-elements appearance, started plodding up and down the middle aisle and chatting in his usual pub style, they began to feel really at home.

After the service the coach party was shepherded into the vicarage, where the vicar's wife, an expert in providing all sorts of beverages and the most delicious sandwiches and home-made cakes and candies at a moment's notice, was waiting behind an almost indecently laden table. For over an hour the coach party and the choir (the bell-ringer had taken the pub-obsessed infant home) mingled and chatted and finally consumed everything on offer. Then the young man in charge of the party bounded on to one of the vicar's peerless Chippendale dining chairs and said what a splendid finale this was to their tour of East Anglian churches.

'Thanks a lot, folks,' he concluded, 'you certainly must come up to our church one of these days for our family service. We've got this terrific group that leads the singing – guitars – drums – the lot. You'll really enjoy it.' Behind me Mr Humphreys erupted into a violent coughing fit and smoke from his pipe billowed all over the place . . .

The rain had stopped as we went out to their coach to see our guests off, and two teenage girls who had been chatting with me assured me that this – what did we call it? – evensong service thing was quite an idea, especially the bit in the vicarage. They were the best cookies they'd ever tasted. The ones they had at the church community centre would take a lot of getting used to after those evensong cookies . . .

17

Silence Is Golden

The big event of the weekend where I was a guest member of yet another village choir was the annual music festival at the community centre. It was a modest enough affair, embracing only a small market town and a cluster of villages, but in the local social calendar it ranked high.

In the church choir section our choir always won the cup. They couldn't help it really. Year after year the chances of the only other entry were zero from the outset, owing to the inclusion in their choir of a lady who had wild imaginings about the beauty of her voice and always referred to herself as a professional. The fact therefore that her alleged voice sounded like a circular saw cutting through a nail carried no weight whatsoever – she was a professional and accordingly the choir's most respected member.

I travelled from London direct to the community centre, and while waiting for our choir to arrive by the local removal van – considered a far more reliable vehicle than the once-a-day bus – I amused myself by listening to the class for solo women's voices. A tall blue-haired lady was on the stage doing her best with something by Vaughan Williams. The only drawback was that she couldn't sing, and the noise she made was swamped by the efforts of someone of the Brute Force and Ignorance School who was blasting a trombone in a nearby room.

Understandably I began to lose interest, and was about to move off when I found myself suddenly cornered by one of the many doting mothers in the hall. Dispensing with introductions, she started to bombard me with details of the sensational voice of her daughter Rosie, a large beefy child of about fourteen, who was reclining across three chairs, gorging from a pound box of chocolates. Mama gave me to understand that if the adjudicator was fair – and they were often grossly unfair – Rosie would win her class hands down, as she had had a great deal of experience. She had indeed carried out some *very* successful professional engagements.

What her version of these would have been I never knew, because at that moment the chocolate consumer was called to the stage. But I heard later that they were quite authentic. On one occasion Rosie had inflicted herself on the inmates of an old people's home who were too infirm to get away, and on another she had sung 'Because' during the interval at the local cinema. The audience there could have escaped, of course, but they were all busy buying ice lollies and salted nuts at the time and didn't notice the threat which was being inflicted upon them.

Despite such a background the biased adjudicator placed Rosie at the bottom of her class. For a moment, Mama was speechless, and she started on me again with terrifying vigour. I kept on saying I was sorry, but it didn't help at all. I was never so glad to see our choir tumble into the hall just in time for their prime time evening appearance on the stage. Squeezing between Mama and the gas radiator against which I had retreated, I made my cowardly escape.

The test piece for the church choir's class was an unmentionable modern anthem by a composer whose sole talent lay in producing discords. Our choir was good at producing discords too, but I don't think they were the kind the composer had in mind, because throughout our performance the adjudicator appeared to be closing his eyes and shuddering. At the end he looked very ill indeed, but he managed to rise to his feet and say we had made a brave try. Words failed him after this, and we all clambered off the stage to the thunderous applause of our supporters, who had got a free ride in our removal van.

As usual our choir members were highly satisfied. The adjudicator hadn't said much, but even if he had slated us right and left, as some rude men had done in the past, it wouldn't have mattered. So long as the circular saw soprano kept up her efforts in the opposing camp the cup was safe with us, and that meant another huge supper at the vicar's expense after the festival.

We now made our way to the tea bar, where an irritable woman stood behind a trestle table pouring out cups of muddy hot water. Her manner, however, in no way dampened the spirits of one of the younger tenors, who was unused to the choir's traditional victories. With a vague idea that he was doing a spot of evangelization he told her that if she wanted to hear some really good singing she should come along to our church on Sunday. This seemed to irritate her even more, and she pushed his muddy hot water at him with such force that half of it slopped in the saucer.

We were trooping out to the removal van when the bomb fell. A member of the rival choir met us in the doorway. He looked pale and bewildered. In the most apologetic tones he told us the awful truth. *His* choir had won the cup.

'I can't understand it,' he admitted shamefacedly. 'We honestly never meant to upset things. That adjudicator must be mad.'

Our choir simply couldn't grasp the situation. The injustice was too unbelievable. And to add insult to injury something had gone wrong with our rivals' hired bus, so we had to offer them a lift home and the best packing cases in our removal van.

Somehow Rosie's furious mother also managed to squeeze herself in with Rosie, who almost landed on my lap with another pound of chocolates. Mama carried on where she had left off earlier. '*Now* can't you see how unjust that adjudicator man is?' she bellowed. 'He ought to be shown up.'

But once again I was saved. The circular saw soprano suddenly appeared on my other side. She'd realized that I was a stranger and the only chorister who hadn't heard from her own lips how good she was. She defeated Rosie's mother with the sheer speed of her attack, and in one breath had introduced herself and explained just how the Royal Opera had missed the soprano of the century.

Conversation soon turned on this afternoon's victory. Yes, she had to admit she was surprised at that – *reely* surprised. She had appeared with the choir, of course – *moral* support was so important, didn't I think? 'But,' she became very confidential, 'I never told them I had developed a dreadful sore throat last night. I dared not risk *forcing* my voice. I just stood on the platform mouthing the words. I never sang a note.'

18

Now He's Upset Everybody

They've got one of these new-age vicars at Hacksaw's village church (I've written before about Hacksaw, my old woodwork master who is organist, choirmaster and bell-ringer here). Like all new-age vicars, this one is naturally keen to alter everything in the parish, from the church services to the central heating, the title of the parish magazine and the colour of the railings around the churchyard. It doesn't matter what it is so long as it's altered. Hacksaw says the rumour is that he's already got the parochial church council in his pocket and is getting away with murder. It's all something to do with dragging the church struggling and protesting into the twenty-first century. And foremost amongst the vicar's most radical aims is that of getting the matins congregation to sing during the service and to sit near each other in Christian fellowship.

The congregation at his recently introduced,

joyous family service which precedes matins *do* sit together and sing most boisterously, songs from big shiny, colourful song books (it's simply not trendy to talk of *hymn* books these days), accompanied by a young woman playing a guitar, replacing organ and choir. But despite the vicar's cajoling (join our happy throng – get with it!) the matins congregation will have none of it. They still don't sing, and they insist on retaining the organ and robed choir, and their special isolated pews. Nothing daunted, however, the vicar continues to be most hopeful that the jolly spirit of his new service will overspill among the matins congregation and that they will eventually see the error of their ways and realize what they are missing. (Hacksaw says they are already *very* aware of what they are missing.) Meanwhile the vicar puts up with them with a brave spirit and cheerful countenance. After all, among them are the bell-ringers, very rare birds in the parish and in great demand at wedding services – and you have to be very careful not to upset such people too much.

Nevertheless, talking of bell ringing, the new-age vicar has already upset the bell-ringers. Until his advent in the parish no vicar or parochial church council had ever dreamed of installing electric lighting in the 500-year-old bell tower. After all, nobody except the ringers ever went near the place, or knew or cared what went on there, provided the bells pealed on time every Sunday and took part in the jollification at numerous weddings, as they'd done for centuries. So the ringers had always plied their ancient craft solely with the aid of two veteran hurricane lamps and a sturdy faith in their sure ability to operate the potentially lethal bell ropes without necessarily seeing them at all clearly. Generations of ringers had looked on the situation as a sort of sacred tradition. They had never been able to see the actual bells other than as a murky silhouette of giant huddled shapes in the perpetual dusk of their chamber.

Then progress, in the shape of the new-age vicar and an eager-to-please church council, had struck. The vicar had the brilliant brainwave of opening the tower to the public as a source of revenue for parish funds. Accordingly, some vandal on the PCC, with absolutely no feeling or respect for tradition, had arranged for the tower to be wired for electricity and all eight bells flooded with a cold clinical blue glare from two chrome-and-plastic-bound fluorescent tubes.

The ringers were devastated. As they pointed out

forcibly and frequently, not only was the action a much resented intrusion into their traditional territory and an affront to the ancient mystic dignity of their bells, it also meant that for the first time in living memory the accumulated dust and debris of the ages was starkly, mercilessly revealed in the alien fluorescent glare and would have to be utterly eliminated before public viewing visits could commence.

During one of my too infrequent visits Hacksaw took me up to the bell chamber to view the disaster. 'There's a mighty lot of work to be done here,' he rumbled, pushing aside pigeon skeletons, draping sheaths of cobwebs and a pile of huge rusty bolts and frayed bell ropes. 'This is all the fault of the vicar and the church council crowd sticking their oar in. Oh, yes, all this'll have to be cleaned up all right, but *they* won't dream of doing it. Oh, no! That'll be left to us. Typical!'

And typically the clearing up in the bell tower was, of course, left to the ringers, and the whole outrageous situation came to the attention of their close allies, the choir, who were also smarting under another modernizing edict from the new-age vicar. The nave of the church had always been more or less heated for the congregation, but in the part of the church where the choir sat they'd never had any heating at all and over the years had come to regard this as a rather prized superior distinction. Up there in the chancel, where grandiose tombs and regal memorials of exalted past worshippers jostled the choirstalls for pride of place, mundane heating apparatus had no place.

But here again the regime of the new-age vicar had trampled on tradition. Plans were in hand to equip the chancel with electric heating, which would mean moving the choirstalls closer together to accommodate modern, starkly functional heaters. According to Hacksaw they were so very starkly modern that they would make the tombs look hopelessly out of place and old fashioned, and were a disgrace apart from the unbelievable necessity of having to move the choirstalls.

'Can you imagine it!' boomed Hacksaw incredulously, 'moving our seats! We've *always* sat there. You get used to singing in a certain place in a certain position. It gives you confidence.'

Most of the choirmen, being ringers also, were doubly indignant about the dastardly lighting and heating machinations of the new-age vicar, and much heated discussion took place each weekend in the bar of 'The Blue Boar'. But, indignant as they were, the protesters were determined not to fall into the trap of approaching the vicar directly. They had learned a lesson from another dissident group in the parish, who had indeed decided to tackle the vicar head-on with their total opposition to whatever he wanted to do.

The vicar, all eager smiles and honeyed words, had invited them to the vicarage, plied them with the most superb sustenance, bare-faced flattery ('The parish owes you the most immense debt of gratitude. Where would the church be without you?') and veiled threats ('The church goes forward or perishes! Yes, of course with all your matchless experience you appreciate that. It's grand you are all so *with* me in our great endeavour. Thank you so much for coming. See you all on Sunday. Don't worry about Karl, he's probably hanging about at the end of the drive. He may look dangerous but he's a very discerning Bull-terrier. He recognizes my friends').

And, quite unexpectedly indeed, it was Karl and his kind who were instrumental in calming the threatening storms gathering around the head of the new-age vicar and returning the parish to its usual state of low key, harmless bickering that so holds parishioners' interest and keeps them happily alive. Early one Sunday morning the vicar was observed uprooting a large NO DOGS sign in the churchyard and replacing it with a larger one stating YOUR WELL-BEHAVED DOG IS WELCOME.

Now, the previous vicar had been, on the whole, a good popular leader but he was nevertheless one of the many priests who, although they might enthusiastically open their churches to special services involving skate boards, bikes and even cars, and provide snacks and drinks at the back of the church and dancing in the aisles and pop concerts in the chancel, nevertheless become very upset at the awful desecration if a cat or dog dares to put its nose inside the doorway of its Creator's house.

'Well, this one's just the opposite,' explained Hacksaw. 'He can't understand why the church is only ever interested in human creatures and has for hundreds of years completely ignored the rest of God's creation. He reckons humans are dead selfish.' Hacksaw scratched his puzzled head. 'I never really thought of it like that – none of us around here did, I suppose, although most of us have dogs and have always been rather narked at the vicar stopping them walking through the churchyard.'

The new-age vicar's first batch of changes in the

parish have now been accomplished. In a blaze of clinical light, the paying visitors to the tower gaze in puzzlement at the ancient giant bells and ask questions like, 'What happens if you don't let go of the rope in time? Do you get pulled up through the ceiling?' And there's alien heat rising amongst the flamboyant tombs and pushed-around choir-stalls in the chancel. Recently, too – even more revolutionary than the introduction of light and heat into the tower and chancel – the first-ever animal blessing service in this church's history has proved an amazing success. As Hacksaw says, you never can tell how things are going to turn out. At long last the lower creation is getting some small recognition in the 'humans only' church.

Karl probably sees it only as a glorious opportunity to discover the hitherto forbidden pleasures of the churchyard with his pal Hacksaw's dog Mortimer, a boisterously friendly sort of all-spare-parts animal with a long, ever-waving whip of a tail that is so very effective in knocking everything off coffee tables in a single swipe.

Rameses, the verger's cat, who has always ruled in the churchyard anyway, is probably quite indifferent to the church's slight turn in his favour. But then Rameses is one of those huge grey regal puff balls who go through life with a small, round turned-up nose and a look of serene superiority. After all, he's always known that he is special and that his Creator knows all about him. At night as he enters the locked church by his secret ways and poses amongst exotic flowers on the high altar he is quite sure that he is special.

19

In The Church if Wet

In my younger choir days one or two choirgirl colleagues made it their urgent business from time to
time to impress on me that I would enjoy life more
and be much more attractive if, apart from giving
myself a break from continually complaining about
the vicar deliberately never choosing any of my
favourite hymns for matins, I would try to be less
formal, particularly in the matter of dress. They
didn't like formality in dress at all. It was absolutely
no use my assuring them that the wearing of an
'office suit' and tie at weekends was infinitely more
natural, comfortable and relaxing for me than don-
ning jeans, 'funny footwear' and T-shirts featuring
blown-up pictures of pop singers and footballers or
advertisements for someone's genuine Olde English
beer. They simply didn't believe me.

Susie was, nevertheless, very keen on the right
kind of informal clothes for the particular informal
occasion. 'Just look at you!' she said accusingly,

as we stood in the middle of a hopelessly isolated Derbyshire village in a blinding sleet storm. 'You look as though you're just off to the City!' I surveyed my saturated, squelching, once smart town shoes, fashionable showerproof mac and the unprotected trouser bottoms of my lounge suit. I shook some of the water from my umbrella, which I dared not open lest it blew inside out. We were on a spring holiday, and waiting for a bus to take us to Sunday evensong at a village church were we were to sing in the choir.

'We can't go clumping into the vestry with dirty great boots and looking like tramps,' I argued. She disregarded my concern, and gave me an exasperated look.

'I can't understand how you always look so *tidy*,' she complained.

Of course, she always talked like that when we were in the country. She liked riding horses, and was never happier than when enveloped in unbelievably shapeless clothes and boots, and wading about in a stableyard up to her knees in mud in the pouring rain.

Anyway, there we stood waiting for the bus which, rumour had it, was supposed to come along about this time. The funny thing about buses – at least, town buses – is that when you are waiting for them in blinding sleet storms they are always late, but when you are aboard them and hoping to get somewhere, they are always early, and keep on loitering round corners in the hope that the buses behind will overtake them and have to collect all the fares. And in the country it's even worse, because the bus you are on is probably the only one for hours, and it has to loiter round corners without the slightest hope of another bus overtaking it.

We had decided on a Derbyshire holiday this year because we were determined to see as much of that beautiful county as possible. Twice before we had tried, but on the first occasion it rained so hard for so long that the beauty spot where we stayed was reduced to a bog and cut off by floods, and on the second occasion the snowstorms were so violent that we had to follow a snow plough in order to get fifty yards up the road to church.

Susie smiled happily from the depths of her suitable country attire. This was a voluminous hooded monstrosity which looked like an old blanket fastened with bits of string and wooden pegs. It almost hid a pair of the biggest rubber boots I'd ever seen.

'I don't know why you're looking so miserable,'

she said, wiping the sleet out of her eyes. 'You don't want to stand there doubled up like an old man of ninety. Stand up and face the weather. It's bracing! It'll do you *good*!'

Just then the bus materialized abruptly, and obligingly sloshed a generous amount of bracing slush all over me. The driver greeted us with a delightful grin. He rubbed his hands together enthusiastically. 'I reckon we're in for a cold snap,' he said. 'I like it. Makes you feel *alive*!' Susie agreed . . .

He was a very obliging driver and stopped the bus specially for us at a side gate of the churchyard which, he explained, gave on to a short cut to the church. The gate was ten feet high, surmounted by a row of vicious rusty spikes and firmly padlocked, so we had the extra pleasure of an invigorating quarter-of-a-mile trudge to the main gate. The sleet was driving a little thicker and harder now, but we were able to sense quite easily where the church lay because the bells had started to ring.

'Don't they sound lovely?' bawled Susie above the shattering sound.

'Lovely,' I mumbled through my chattering teeth, as I fell over a half-buried gravestone, but I don't think she heard me.

'You needn't *sulk*,' she remonstrated. 'It seems to me you're not enjoying *anything* today. Whatever is the *matter* with you?'

But once on familiar ground in the choir vestry, I bucked up tremendously. The vicar introduced us to the choir, and everyone was extremely friendly. As I prepared to robe, I was about to hang my jacket on a large nail in the stone wall. Immediately a choirman put his arm across it in friendly warning.

'Don't put it there,' he said. 'The wall's got no plaster on it, and the stone's flaking. It makes a terrible mess of your clothes.' I thanked him for his forethought as I watched him hang *his* jacket on the very nail I had been about to use. He noticed my puzzlement.

'I always hang my things here,' he explained. 'They get absolutely *filthy*. I have to brush 'em down after service. It's the stone, y'see. It's flaking . . .'

I thanked him again, rolled up my jacket and placed it on the floor in the corner. There was only a thick layer of dust there, and I felt it would be much easier to remove than the flaking stone.

As the choir processed up the aisle singing the opening hymn, I realized that the weather had had little effect on the size of the congregation. The church was filled to capacity. Here indeed was a faithful flock. Everybody had carefully spread their soaking macs over the backs of their pews so that they could drain off all over the feet of the people in the pew behind. As we entered the chancel, through an ancient black chancel screen, the joyous volume of noise from the congregation reduced to a whisper. The screen was so thick that it almost cut us off from sight and sound of the nave, and we were in a little world of our own. It was a familiar little world. As we reached our places someone immediately passed along a tube of peppermints, someone else knocked over a pile of hymn books, and the organist started to adjust the mirror over his console. It is a weakness that many organists have. The mirror never seems to be in the right position, and however satisfied he might be after about half-an-hour of intermittent fiddling at matins, an organist always has to re-adjust it at evensong.

I had an unmistakable feeling that everyone was thoroughly enjoying the service. I doubt whether many of the congregation heard the anthem – but then, congregations don't hear anthems where they have ancient thick choir screens – and I'm certain that no one in the choir heard the sermon – but,

20

All Donations Thankfully Received

For a considerable time everything had been going right in the parish. By some extraordinary fluke the vicar had been choosing hymns for services which everybody liked, no one had complained about the choirboys chewing sweets throughout evensong, not a single child had been thrown out of the Sunday school for vandalism, and the only man who understood the workings of the evil-tempered church boiler had not made his usual monthly threat to resign. Even the members of the church council had been agreeing with each other.

The vicar felt completely out of her depth, and absolutely unprepared to deal with the situation. Not only had she received no complaints and encountered no opposition from anyone, but last Sunday a woman who had sat in the pew under the pulpit every matins for twenty-five years and never failed to attack every sermon she'd ever heard, had actually rung the vicar to say how much comfort and joy she had received from her latest offering.

The whole thing was getting quite out of hand.

And then, like a sandstorm in the desert, there arose the case of the new choir cassocks.

I had been a guest in the choir of the frowning, grime-veiled London church on a number of occasions, and when I entered the vestry on this my latest visit I sensed immediately that something more than the usual unholy uproar was afoot.

A gigantic, drooping-moustached gentleman, who usually bellowed bass down the back of my neck and always seemed to be passing a bag of liquorice allsorts up and down the choirstalls during the sermon, rolled across to me, his usually beaming face now purple with anger. He was accompanied by his constant companion, a small red-haired tenor called Fred. Both were arrayed in new single-breasted black cassocks which, not being buttoned up, flapped aimlessly around them.

'What about these?' the gigantic bass appealed to me. 'There's a new man in the congregation – only been here about five years – who thinks we should have new cassocks, so he sees the vicar and goes out and buys 'em. Just like that.'

'Just like that,' said Fred.

'We're going to call a choir committee meeting about this, pretty sharp,' thundered the gigantic bass. 'The choir weren't even *consulted*.'

'That's right,' agreed Fred, eagerly, 'not even *consulted*.'

'We don't like the colour, for a start,' pursued the gigantic bass, cornering me between a broken iron heating stove and a disreputable-looking piano. 'We've *never* had black cassocks here.'

'Always been a greeny blue,' explained Fred, gazing morosely at his new garment. 'Rather unusual, really. I think that when we first had 'em they were supposed to be just blue. I think . . .'

His companion drowned him. 'The vicar's not getting away with this – committee meeting at my place, straight after matins.'

'Single-breasted, too,' said Fred. 'Imagine how long it'll take to do up all those little buttons. We'll have to come earlier.'

'The vicar will have to wait,' amended the gigantic bass. 'When she's done up the three buttons on her double-breasted cassock she'll have to wait while we do up the fifteen on our single-breasted ones.'

Four or five more choirmen had now arrived and were standing aghast before their cassock pegs, on each of which hung a brand-new cassock.

'What's the meaning of this? Where's my cassock?' exploded our gentleman, who was carrying a copy of Mendelssohn's 'Elijah' and *The News of the World*.

'New cassocks. Someone's bought 'em. We've got to wear 'em,' explained Fred.

The questioner reverently placed his *News of the World* across two pegs and flung 'Elijah' on top of a cupboard. 'I don't know how we *stand* it,' he fumed, 'I don't know what we're coming to.'

'The trouble is, we're not appreciated,' said the gigantic bass. 'They don't understand a good choir here. Pearls before swine. First the vicar stops us doing anthems because she says they're too long . . .'

'It was the twenty-minute one the other Sunday that did it,' put in Fred.

'. . . then the church council cuts the beer money for the annual outing, and now,' – the gigantic bass's mind seemed to boggle at the unparalleled insult – 'we've got to wear new cassocks.'

'Black ones, too,' said Fred, 'with all those little buttons down the front.'

We stood, a suddenly stunned circle, contemplating a future blighted by the torture of the little black buttons.

The door leading from the church swung open vigorously and two men entered, one giving the unmistakable impression of driving the other. The driven one was a small nervous-looking type, who appeared to be searching desperately for a way of escape. The driver was a lordly, expansive, pin-striped gentleman whom I knew to be the vicar's warden. His great joy in life was to collar visitors the moment they ventured inside the church door, announce with quiet dignity who he was, and firmly hustle them into a conducted tour of the building. Indeed, he had devoted a great deal of his time for many years to hammering home his wildly inaccurate history of the church, and was considered a great authority.

The reluctant gentleman was obviously a visitor, and the vicar's warden was just as obviously determined to show him everything in the church, even the choir. After explaining that the vestry was a later addition to the church (he waved his arms at the barn-like, late Victorian solidity and proclaimed rapturously 'Georgian, you see. Very fine') he stood well back from us and said, 'And that's our choir.'

To show that, although tremendously lordly, he was also very friendly and willing to speak to just anyone, he remarked to the vestry at large, 'So you've got new cassocks then. Very nice, very nice. Good, good.' And when his words met with that curious lack of response with which so many of his words usually were met, his friendliness continued unabated, and he stood a little further back and said 'Splendid. Splendid.'

The effect was rather spoilt for him when the vestry door opened abruptly behind him and pushed him forward most unceremoniously. A little old man, wearing a long, extremely dirty raincoat, and with his trouser bottoms tied round with boot-laces, entered the vestry and walked across to a cupboard where he divested himself of the raincoat and put on a rusty black gown and an extremely crumpled and frayed university hood. He made no attempt to remove the bootlaces and took no notice whatsoever of the fuming choir who, in turn, took no notice whatsoever of him.

'And that's our organist,' said the vicar's warden.

The organist *never* took any notice of the choir. He didn't believe in choirs, especially this one. He just couldn't believe that the congregation couldn't sing without the choir. In fact he couldn't visualize *any* congregation standing dumb when he was play-ing a hymn, because he knew that he played so well. All the choir did was to upset him right through the service by singing in front of the organ, or behind the organ, or much louder and flatter than the organ, and then they upset him again after the service by kicking up such a din in the vestry that it quite spoilt his beautiful voluntary. He didn't like the choir at all.

He couldn't help hearing the down-to-earth remarks that rose from the group of choirmen around the cassock pegs. Again and again he caught the words 'Resign' and 'St Jude's would be pleased to have us' and 'What about the Methodists?' He smiled discreetly as he climbed into the organ loft. In his mind's eye he saw the choirstalls beautifully empty. He couldn't help feeling happy . . .

On leaving the vestry, the vicar's warden had driven his visitor into the Sunday school to show him what was going on there. A football match was, in fact, going on just then, and as the two passed a glass partition, the ball misguidedly found its way through the glass and on to the head of the visitor. The visitor said that it was quite all right and that he wasn't hurt, and scuttled thankfully away.

The vicar's warden, thunderous, investigated and found that the culprit was a sturdy urchin who had never treated him with anything like the proper respect when he had ordered him out of the vicar's pear trees, or out of the cupboard at the end of the church, where one flick of a switch could plunge the whole place into darkness. He ordered the urchin out of the Sunday school there and then, and told him a letter to his parents would be following very shortly. Two little girls who came into the classroom looked at him uncertainly. He smiled at them graciously. He felt very happy.

The vicar walked up the centre aisle of the church to the vestry. Everybody smiled at her. They all seemed so happy. Once again, not one member of the congregation had waylaid her in the porch with a complaint or a downright threat. She was becoming more and more disturbed.

She entered the vestry. Her expert eye took in the grim, accusing faces bunched together before her. The gigantic bass and Fred strode forward threateningly, their new unbuttoned cassocks flapping behind them like the wings of great birds of ill omen.

Then the vicar smiled her famous, winning smile and visibly relaxed. Like the organist and the vicar's warden, she felt happy. Things were getting back to normal.

21

Who Are These Like
Stars Appearing?

It was a very small village indeed. The guide books never mentioned it, and its church was well and truly ignored by all the 'arty' books on the churches of England. During its five hundred years the church had been restored a dozen times and still looked as if it was falling down. It was of no architectural merit whatsoever, contained no fine brasses or marbles, and had never been even remotely connected with a single famous or infamous person. Even Oliver Cromwell hadn't thought it worthwhile plundering. And the present-day villagers didn't mind at all.

The night that I arrived in their midst, on a visit to a twice-removed cousin, was a very outstanding one. It was the night of the choir's winter beetle drive. For as long as anyone could remember, the choir had held a function in the church hall. For years it had taken the form of a whist drive, but lately difficulties had arisen. The majority of the choir's supporters only revived their knowledge of the game on this one occasion each year, and the small number of those who were regular and serious players appeared to become extraordinarily cross and even unfriendly when well-meaning partners of the once-a-year school continually trumped their tricks. So, to avoid the danger of open violence, the whist drives had given place to beetle drives.

No one could forget how to play beetle. You just kept on rolling the dice and drawing beetles on a card full of little blank squares. The idea was to finish the drawing first and bawl out 'Beetle', because this gave you the maximum points, and stopped everyone else from completing their beetles.

My twice-removed cousin, who had taken me along to the village hall, immediately sought out the organist, a happy-looking, plump, middle-aged type, who was meditating over a large rusty oil-stove which appeared to be leaking all over the floor. We stood in a pool of paraffin, and fell to talking about choirs. The organist explained that he really looked forward to the beetle drive, because it was one of the few occasions during the entire year when he met the whole choir together. 'You see,' he explained, 'there are those who hardly ever come to matins, and there are those who hardly ever come to evensong – and, of course, there are those who hardly ever come to Friday night practice.' Then there were those who hardly ever came at all.

But the rules of membership were very reasonable. You were considered a member of the choir as long as you turned up at the great festivals, and when anyone connected with the choir was getting christened, married or buried. You were definitely expected to turn up then. And, naturally, at the annual beetle drive.

An imposing lady in a large green dress covered with red buttons and pictures of French landmarks now planted herself in front of us in the paraffin oil, and ordered us to take our seats as the drive was about to begin.

So we seated ourselves round little baize-topped tables, and started furiously to throw the dice. In the manner of such tables they were very unsteady and sloped at all angles but, also in the manner of such tables, the dice were effectively prevented from rolling off by being trapped in the numerous moth-holes in the baize.

After a number of hilarious games, feverishly drawing demented-looking insects and hollering 'Beetle', I found myself partnering the large lady in the French-landmark dress. She was obviously one of those self-appointed welcomers of strangers to the parish, who lurk at the back of so many churches. Their job is to corner you and make you feel wanted.

She now gave me her undivided attention. She forgot about our beetle to such an extent that, when our opponents suddenly shouted 'Beetle' and triumphantly waved a completed insect, ours had only got as far as a headless body with no legs. She was very kind to me, and made me feel so much a part of things. Already she'd found out that I was an alto. She smiled a huge terrifying smile, and told me that I was the living image of her dear old grandfather, who had lived till he was ninety-four. She remembered him especially, she said, because he also was an alto. When she was a very little girl, her father had explained to her what an alto voice was. He'd been rather obliged to do this because she had worried about her grandfather, firmly believing that he suffered from some throat complaint and couldn't help making a noise like that.

At the next game, I found my partner was an elderly gentleman who was rolling a microscopic cigarette, which contained so little tobacco that, when lighted, it caught fire and burned his fingers.

He was, however, a very able partner, and helped me win my only complete beetle of the evening. We had now reached the half-way mark in the contest, and this called for a break for tea and the sale of raffle tickets.

The vicar, who had just arrived and had failed to slip past the choirman on the door without paying (year after year he pitted his wits against this particular choirman, but he always failed), started to hold up the prizes which could be won in the raffle. Everyone exclaimed appreciatively at the sight of a large basket of fruit – everyone except my partner. 'I won the basket of fruit last year,' he grated at me. 'Don't be taken in! It's padded with paper underneath – not two bobs' worth of fruit in it.'

As the prizes were shown, the enthusiasm increased, and tickets were being sold by the dozen. Finally, the vicar displayed a great box of green and blue soap together with yellow bath salts, and my partner, who was rolling another cigarette and spilling the tobacco in my tea, informed me in a confidential whisper that could be heard from one end of the hall to the other, 'Vicar's wife donated that. One of her Christmas presents she didn't want.'

I've never won a beetle drive, and this occasion

was no exception. At the end of the drive, most of my beetles had progressed no further than one leg and one eye, but, contrary to custom, I did win a raffle prize. It was only a third, but I felt quite bucked as I approached the table where the vicar was supervising the prize-giving. The first and second winners chose what they wanted, and then the vicar shook hands with me and invited me to take my pick from the two remaining items. He said I could have either the home-perm set or the nylon scrubbing brush.

The fourth prize-winner was the organist's Boxer dog, Siegfried. The organist always put Siegfried's name on one of his tickets. Siegfried didn't know he'd won. He was cautiously licking up the paraffin oil round the stove. But I often wonder what he did with the home-perm set.

22

Plenty More Fish in the Sea

They've never heard of such an innovation as a quiet time before the service at a church I know in an otherwise most peaceful riverside town in Oxfordshire. It is a firmly established practice, dating back to the eighteenth century, when music in the church was provided by a bass viol and two or three other assorted instruments, that exactly half-an-hour before a service begins there should be a warm-up of the music to be heard later at the service. It is also an unassailable tradition that the bell-ringers should start ringing at precisely the same time. Today, of course, the organ provides the music, and the present organist enthusiastically carries on the revered practice of the pre-service warm-up. Indeed, his enthusiasm has taken him a number of steps further than his predecessors, and he not only plays music to be heard at the service but also a great deal of music that never has been, and is not at all likely to be, heard at the service or anywhere else in a civilized society.

The bell-ringers still ring the same bells as did their eighteenth-century forebears, and again are most enthusiastic in keeping up a great tradition of getting everyone out of bed on Sunday morning. A Victorian restorer, for some sadistic reason, louvred the church wall between the bell tower and the nave so that the sound of the bells can be heard as deafeningly inside the church as outside, and when, in the half hour before the service, the organist backs up the mighty efforts of the ringers with his unique artistry, the atmosphere in the church is, in the words of the vicar's warden, who is a percussion player in the town band, 'not 'alf stunning'.

Of course it means that the many members of the congregation who come early to the service in order to have a good gossip at the back of the church can't hear what they're talking about unless they bawl at each other at the tops of their voices, and this they cheerfully do, raising the mind-blowing din ('the glad sound,' according to the vicar, a serenely smiling lady) to the level of that in a main-line railway station in the rush hour, accompanied by a monster performance of the 1812 overture.

This evidence of 'cheerful Christian togetherness' (another of the vicar's quaint terms) continues until the very moment of the choir's entry into the chancel, at which point everybody scrambles for their seats, the vicar cries, 'A very warm welcome to you all,' and the choir leads off with a vigorous rendering of one of the vicar's favourite marching hymns, all about getting mixed up in mighty conflicts and smiting all and sundry.

I like everything about this church, particularly about the choir, which is large, enthusiastic and friendly. I sing in it whenever I am in the vicinity, and am looked upon as a regular member.

When I arrived in the vestry on a recent Sunday evening after an absence of some weeks, I immediately realized that something out of the ordinary was afoot because the uproar in the place was even greater than usual. Indeed it was almost drowning out the stunning efforts of the combined organ and bells, and the crush of choir members getting in each other's way trying to clamber into their robes seemed to have at least doubled itself. I couldn't get near the cassock cupboard for a time, but it didn't matter because someone had taken the robes I generally wore, and I was lucky to secure a venerable cassock which hung behind the broom cupboard door and had for years been used exclusively by the verger when he had some dirty work to do in the tower or in the stoke-hole. I brushed it down gently so that its coating of coke dust wouldn't fly everywhere, and gladly accepted a proffered piece of string from a small round choirboy with spiky hair and extraordinarily large trainers, who stood watching me critically.

'You have to tie it round the middle,' he explained. 'It's got no buttons.' I thanked him for his kind consideration, and he dived behind the vestry piano and dragged out what looked like an uncared-for Victorian nightshirt with wings.

'It's the Angel Gabriel's surplice,' he said. 'He wears it at the Christmas pageant. My mum hasn't washed it yet for next Christmas but it'll look all right on you just for tonight, if I take the wings off.'

He proceeded to undo a series of large safety pins, and smartly shook the surplice free of Gabriel's wings, some miscellaneous sweet wrappers and an indignant-looking spider. 'There,' he said, handing it to me, beaming, 'how's that?'

'Fine, lovely,' I enthused, 'but what's all the fuss about?'

My small round helper looked down at his large

trainers and peeled a blob of bubble gum off one of them. He examined it minutely. 'I wondered where that had gone,' he said in a relieved voice. 'I had to get rid of it when I had a solo bit to sing in the Te Deum this morning. I thought I stuck it under the hymn book shelf. It must have fallen off . . .'

'About all this fuss,' I recalled him, 'what's going on?'

'Oh, it's Julia and George,' he confided mysteriously, popping the bubble gum into his mouth. 'They're sort of getting married.'

A well-known voice rumbled behind me out of the rising din. 'Go light the candles,' it commanded the small round one, 'and change the left-hand one. It dropped grease all down one side this morning and there's a mess on the altar carpet.' The gentleman with the large voice was our large bass soloist. 'This is not going to help,' he pronounced, 'this business of Julia and George getting engaged.'

I was rather at a loss for an answer to this. Julia was our soprano soloist, a delightful girl with a delightful voice, and George could sing tenor quite well if he knew the tune. I couldn't see what was wrong.

'I reckon we'll lose at least a half dozen of the

lads now she's done this,' pursued the big bass, cuffing a choirboy who was trying to park his skateboard in the cassock cupboard.

'Who?' I said.

'Julia, of course,' he rumbled. 'While she only wanted to mess about with horses and go skiing and sing in the choir, the lads all felt they had a chance with her, but now she's gone and got herself engaged – well, it won't help the choir, will it?'

Just then the vicar, an energetic and sprightly type, sprang on to the piano stool and shouted that she was sure everyone was going to enjoy the very special evensong which was at the moment ten minutes late in starting, and that she'd see everyone at the continuing engagement celebrations at the vicarage immediately after the service.

I shall long remember that evensong. It was one of the most enjoyable I have ever taken part in – and the longest. (After the singing of a particularly popular hymn on special occasions such as Christmas or Easter, or on reports of parishioners getting engaged or having babies or getting a place in the local football team, the vicar is apt to announce, 'Well, we all enjoyed singing that so much, let's sing it again.') In the great tradition of this particular church all the music, including the repeated hymns, was sung in a manner fit to raise the roof, and culminated in a glorious, rumbustious performance of a twenty-page anthem by Goss. Who could ask for more?

Afterwards at the vicarage everyone congratulated the happy couple, and in less than three-quarters of an hour had entirely consumed the vast amount of food and drink provided by the vicar's sister, who can never sing a note in tune and absolutely adores the choir. As the party broke up, the bass soloist was still voicing his fears about the likely loss of a number of younger male members of the choir.

But life goes on. Some months later I was back in the choir again. Julia sang the soprano solo in the anthem as beautifully as ever, but the soprano in the following quartet was someone I'd not seen before. She was a delightful girl with a delightful voice who, I learned later, had recently moved into the parish with her father and mother. She likes messing about with horses and skiing and, of course, singing in the choir.

All the young men are still in the choir, as keen as ever. Indeed, there seem to be one or two extra ones these days . . .

23

Hark the Glad Sound

A Christmas spent in a small Dorset town gave me a wonderful opportunity of joining the parish church choir in their traditional Christmas Eve carol singing at the local hospital.

This delightfully ramshackle Victorian monstrosity, affectionately known as the slaughterhouse, was held in the very highest esteem by the townsfolk. Like the parish church and the gasworks, it was part of their heritage, and they made strenuous efforts to oppose all attempts by the Department of Health and Social Security to close it. They made even more strenuous efforts to ensure that none of them, however ill, entered the place.

Generally, therefore, a large number of beds remained permanently vacant, but lately business had improved. Outside the hospital the road was very narrow, and the Council had embarked on a vast programme of improvements. This had gone on for months, appearing to consist solely of a large waterlogged hole, carefully surrounded each night by half-a-dozen unlit oil lamps. Unwary travellers then drove headlong into it, and had only to be trundled a few yards into the hospital.

On this Christmas Eve, as was the cherished custom, the choir arrived at the tradesmen's entrance fully robed, and fully half an hour late. We were greeted by the Matron who was obviously brimming with the seasonal spirit of goodwill. 'Wipe your feet,' she rasped encouragingly, and placed her ample form solidly in the way until we had done so. We then followed her down a series of arctic passages smelling of disinfectant and onions, to our first port of call, a ward full of elderly ladies.

We filed in, smiling and murmuring Merry Christmases to the patients, who greeted us with dignified silence, their dear old faces transformed into masks of maniacal fury.

A choirman next to me whispered that this was really quite understandable. To accommodate us a nurse had just turned off the ward television at the most exciting part of the special Christmas Eve gangster film, in which a mob of maladjusted layabouts were beating up a policeman in Big Lou's Pool Room. Bravely we assembled round a Christmas tree in the middle of the floor, and I noticed we had been joined by two new characters. One was a large yellow cat who gave the unmistakable impression that he was laughing at us, and the other was a middle-aged lady who reminded me strongly of a pencil. I gathered that she was a Miss Selina and was kindly to accompany us on her violin.

The first carol was 'Good King Wenceslas', and as the choir possessed three tenors who all thought they were indispensable the part of the King was sung in triplicate. This unfortunately rather over-awed the page boy, causing him to miss altogether his soprano complaint about the dirty night. However, we all trickled in gradually, and attention was drawn away from the boy by Miss Selina, who was setting everyone's teeth on edge with her unique accompaniment of the famous carol.

We followed with two or three more well-known carols, in which to my surprise the Matron joined. She was standing behind me, but I recognized immediately that forceful 'Wipe your feet' roar as it asserted itself, speeded our flagging tempo, and with the utmost ease flattened us a tone per verse.

Finally we came to Miss Selina, who announced coyly that she would now play a 'Christmas piece'. I am not a competent judge of violin playing, and I don't quite know what she was trying to do, but it was interesting to note that during the performance the oldest patient had to be forcibly restrained from walking out – and the yellow cat rolled all over the floor in a wild ecstasy.

Our reception at the next stop – the men's ward – was far less violent. Here the patients had been able to see the end of the TV gangster film, and when we arrived were peacefully settling down to sleep.

Of course, we soon altered all that when we opened up with 'Silent Night'. Miss Selina's violin just didn't blend with our voices, especially as she was playing 'O Come, All ye Faithful' for the first few bars. There was a sudden movement right down the ward as patients began to prop themselves up or bury their heads under the bedclothes. We saw no more of the buried ones, but the rest seemed genuinely interested. It was indeed encouraging to overhear a man in a bed near me call out to his neighbour that this looked like being a very funny turn. The yellow cat now attached himself to me, fondling round my ankles and purring. Perhaps he sensed that I was a cat lover, or perhaps my alto voice intrigued him. Anyway, he still seemed to be laughing. The choir soon got under way with another selection of carols sung in our usual swashbuckling, devil-may-care manner – and with more success this time. The Matron had threatened to take command again, but during the singing of 'The First Noel' had been urgently called down the ward to a very obstreperous patient. He was a well-known music teacher and was threatening to throw a fit and sue the Department of Health and Social Security.

After inflicting ourselves on two more wards we were thanked by the Matron in her most threatening tone. She handed us some curious basin-like cups full of alleged tea, and having disposed of this, we were allowed to go.

As we reached the exit there approached us a large genial porter who really radiated the spirit of Christmas goodwill. Beaming all over his face he asked us kindly to stand aside to let the stretcher bearers through. They'd just caught another customer down the hole in the road.

24

The Lurker in the Supermarket

I was standing bewildered in a supermarket surrounded by 'unbeatable offers' and 'gigantic bargains'. Mountains of detergents were 50 pence off, and gallons of orange squash were 'unrepeatable'. A gentleman on a loudspeaker kept telling me that I should make sure of getting my free sachet of shampoo with someone's heavenly-tasting toothpaste; and a large banner over a counter bearing a mass of chocolate of unknown origin, assured me that this was the finest I could lay my tongue to.

Actually, I wasn't looking for bargains; I was lost. My aunt, with whom I was staying on a short country holiday, had asked if I'd call at the nearby town's new supermarket for some bacon and eggs and cat-food. She said she'd be most grateful if I'd do this for her, as it would save her for a little longer from the clutches of the new lady church-worker who always lurked behind the detergents on Saturday afternoons, in an effort to waylay the more elusive members of the parish church congregation. The lady-worker's birdlike face continually beamed with goodwill, and she was brimming with ideas for good works which she liberally distributed to others to carry out. She was therefore held in the greatest respect, and avoided whenever possible.

Not that the craftiest efforts of the congregation spared them for long. The vicar was also brimming with ideas for good works, and it was well known that if the lady-worker didn't catch you, the vicar would. This, of course, explained why Sunday by Sunday half the congregation could be observed unobtrusively shuffling out of church by the side door while the vicar and lady-worker were shaking hands at the main door.

It was agreed, however, that only the choir and organist were successful in avoiding any involvement whatsoever. Whenever the choir were approached regarding good works, there always appeared to be dozens of mysterious practices in the offing which would take up every evening of the week. No one quite knew what they did at these practices, because they'd sung the same chants for forty years, and always refused to learn a new hymn.

As for the organist, he lived in a world of his own. An almost invisible wisp of a man, dressed from a jumble sale, he was forever darting all over the place at a breathtaking rate, carrying wads of tattered organ voluntaries. Neither the vicar nor the lady-worker ever succeeded in burdening him with commissions for good works, because half the time he didn't even recognize who was speaking to him. Indeed, judging by his gloriously individualistic organ accompaniments, he seldom even recognized the choir.

I thought I'd dithered long enough in the shadow of the great detergent mountains, so I allowed myself to be borne along by the enveloping tide of housewives who nudged me gently with wire baskets, kicked my ankles, or simply barged me out of the way by brute force. My reasoning was that sooner or later I should be carried towards the counters displaying eggs and bacon and cat-food, and I might be able to grab something in passing. This I entirely accomplished, although I found it rather difficult to protect my purchases as I'd left my carrier bag in the bus and had forgotten to arm myself with a wire basket. However, a kindly young lady at the pay desk gave me a carrier, and I was about to make my escape when I felt a steel grip on my arm.

I turned guiltily, as we all do when steel grips

are laid on our arms, to confront the lady-worker. Naturally she was beaming. Was my aunt with me? No! What a pity! She wanted a *very* important word in her ear. She'd got *such* a thrilling idea about a Christmas pageant – dozens of costumes to run up. My aunt was clever with her needle, was she not? No sense in hanging about! Things had to get moving *now*! And what about me? Would I be down again for Christmas? because if so . . .

I said firmly that unfortunately I wouldn't, but that I should be singing in the choir on the morrow. Mention of the choir seemed to dampen even her enthusiasm, but she soon recovered and explained that her nephew, who had recently joined the choir, was under-manager of the supermarket, and that she would introduce me at once. 'Follow me,' she ordered brightly, and plunged back into the terrifying mass of humanity and detergents.

How she reached the far end of the shop I shall never know. I became completely cut off at the butcher's department, where I took shelter by a large pillar which was plastered with adverts for sausages and pork pies which the management thoroughly recommended, and a notice about watching out for pick-pockets for which the management could not be held responsible.

Within a few minutes I was rescued by the lady-worker, who returned with a breathless and battered nephew.

'Where did you *get* to?' she enquired, not unkindly. 'Men will *dither* so. It's the same when they tackle a job at the church. *Drive* is what you all need! *Drive!*'

It was all drive in that parish. On the way to church on the Sunday morning the lady-worker's nephew told me that the vicar, who had been the prime mover – in fact, the only mover – in the churchyard clearance scheme, had recently overshot the churchyard and driven a bulldozer through someone's garden wall, and the lady-worker was successfully driving everyone to distraction and to other churches.

You could sense the nervousness in the congregation as they dodged furtively into church and scuttled to their seats in dark corners and behind pillars. In the vestry, however, the whole atmosphere was different. The choir was so large that it was like being in the supermarket all over again, but without the urgency of the bargain hunting. There was the calm, friendly air of people who knew what they were about, of independent people who would not be driven. The vicar, however, had been known to interpret this as an air of open defiance. But he appreciated his choir. They were, he said, an ever present challenge to him, to keep him from relaxing even for a moment in his fight against ignorance and apathy within the church. He would not do without them.

25

Just Picture It

George and I were taking down the numerous venerable choir photographs that crowded the vestry walls of the village church where George is organist and choirmaster. The vestry was due for its once-a-century clean-up and redecoration, and had to be cleared of the unbelievable accumulation of choir memorabilia that had engulfed it since the last occasion, two world wars away, that a paint brush had touched its walls.

George wiped the grime from a large faded sepia photograph of the choir as it was in the days just after Queen Victoria died. 'Look at that!' he exclaimed enviously, 'sixteen men and two dozen boys. Those were the days! We had the kids lining up to join the choir then. They were paid half-a-crown a quarter, and were fined tuppence every time they turned up at church with filthy boots and black finger nails or made a mess of the solo at matins. When it came to pay day some of them had been fined so much that they didn't get any money at all, and even owed the church money, but they still came to choir. It was like being in a gang. They loved it. The men in the choir didn't get paid. They sang simply for the sheer joy of it – they had choir practice in the back room of "The Bull at the Gate" every Friday night and it was much more popular than darts and dominoes.'

George pointed to a large bewhiskered figure in the centre of the photograph. 'There's my grandad. He was a bass and was in the choir for so many years that he collected four long-service presentation cups, three inscribed beer mugs, two chiming clocks, a garden shed full of tools, and a weekend in Paris. He was really enthusiastic about the choir. He could never read music but you could hear his voice for miles.'

We carried on removing the photographs and stacking them wherever we could find room under the back pews, which already harboured numerous relics of the past – moth-eaten hassocks, chipped flower vases, backless hymn books and the usual interesting collection of forgotten umbrellas, gloves, scarves and children's toys. 'Of course,' resumed George, 'as you know, it's much harder getting men to join the choir these days – you can talk women into it easily enough but not men – and the funny thing is that the men who *do* show an interest are those who shouldn't be allowed within a mile of a choir.'

'So you do get a few enquiries?' I said.

'A few too many,' confirmed George. 'They're the ones who say they used to be in the choir as school kids but have been so busy since that they haven't had the time, but now they'd like to pick up the threads again. The trouble is, these volunteers are always so nice and so *keen* – but that doesn't help at all when they sing everything an octave lower and don't realize it. We have to get rid of them.'

'And that puts you in an awkward spot,' I sympathized.

George grinned. 'Well, you're used to being put in awkward spots when you've anything to do with the choir. It's normally to do with running battles with the vicar about hymn tunes – but I must say the vicar here can be very helpful when it comes to re-routing potential choristers who can't sing.'

Apparently the vicar, with the irresistibility of an attacking tiger, pounces on the would-be chorister and assures him that he is the very person – for whom he has been searching desperately for months

– to concentrate on worthy objects like preparing the ground for beautifying the churchyard with flowering shrubs, or taking over the operating of the ailing obsolete church boiler, or acting as official welcomer at the 8 o'clock Sunday morning service when everyone tries to get in and out of the church without recognizing anyone else.

The vicar is almost always successful. After half-an-hour of his out-of-this-world, glowing enthusiasm and overflowing Christian togetherness his victims are so eager to get on with digging holes in the churchyard, stoking boilers and forcibly shaking hands with the 8 o'clock congregation that they forget all about their desire to join the choir, and never have time to think of it again. But as with all things, there are exceptions, and the case of Big Hector was a glaring example of the vicar's parishioner-processing formula failing spectacularly. Big Hector, an elderly but vigorous bachelor, had suddenly burst upon the parish having recently retired from a world-wide career of doing everything everywhere fantastically successfully. He was now staying at the vicarage prior to moving to a nearby village, where he'd purchased the biggest local 'much-sought-after Victorian residence with many original features', which even now was being transformed into an even bigger much-sought-after Victorian residence with many original features.

In the meantime Big Hector had decided to join our choir, and having learned of the forthcoming redecoration and refurbishment of the choir vestry, resolved to finance and oversee the whole operation. Gatecrashing a choir practice which was entirely unprepared for his debut into parish musical life, he explained his plans at length, and when the stunned singers eventually got round to actual singing, demonstrated enthusiastically that, like former volunteers, he was innocent of the faintest musical ability and possessed a singing voice resembling that of an enraged rogue elephant.

The situation was intriguing. 'I wonder how the vicar is going to help the choir get rid of *this* one?' I asked George.

'Get rid!' he echoed incredulously. 'Big Hector is the answer to the vicar's prayers. This man is insisting on *paying* for the entire vestry renovation job. It means that the vicar and the church council won't have to carry on arguing for hours and hours about the lowest knock-down price they'll be willing to pay for the work. Big Hector is the kind of singer the vicar appreciates and will welcome into the choir with open arms.'

'But has he *heard* Big Hector singing?' I queried.

George smiled grimly. 'Oh yes, he heard him at choir practice the other night. His enthusiasm was spectacular. We had his usual "Great! Splendid! Wow – Jolly good!" bit, and then he said how fortunate and blessed we were to have a new choir member with such an interesting, yea uniquely beautiful, joyous voice. I tell you, the vicar's surpassed himself this time! Big Hector is firmly in the choir and there's nothing we can do about it.'

Meanwhile the refurbishment of the choir vestry sped ahead. Traditionally the vestry could now have looked forward to soporific months of gentle dust-laden chaos punctuated by regular special meetings of the church council to 'review progress' of the work. Everything that went on in the parish was always regularly reviewed at special church council meetings – nice, cosy social evenings at the vicarage, where the vicar's wife's catering made serving on the council well worthwhile. Big Hector knew nothing of the special meeting tradition. Under his ever watchful eye the work, much extended, was startlingly, splendidly completed before the church council had even considered a date for the first special vestry refurbishment meeting.

While the work on the choir vestry had been in

200

progress the choir had been moved into the bell-ringers' chamber at the back of the church, a dim, cave-like place which barely accommodated the six ringers, all of whom were on the large or very large side. As George remarked, it was hardly ideal but it was a case of any port in a storm, and Sunday by Sunday the singers doggedly faced a constant danger of being flayed alive by the thrashing bell ropes as the ringers carried on regardless with the traditional welcoming peal. And so, miraculously without damage to life and limb, came the Sunday morning when the choir were introduced to their revitalized vestry.

They straggled through the doorway and gaped around at the brightness and openness, the pale polished floor, the gleaming windows, the rows of shining brass hangers and adjustable steel music shelves, the latest state-of-the-art lighting – and the ultimate violent shock, the sleek brand-new electronic piano.

The tenor soloist, who always sat next to the vicar and annoyed him by continually sucking throat sweets with noisy relish throughout the service, was first to speak. 'Where is everything?' His neighbour looked bewildered. 'This is a different place.' He crossed to where the new metal shelves extended along the whole of one wall. He peered through them at the gleaming, primrose painted wall to where formerly there existed a long battered board carrying a series of large bent nails and one or two twisted hooks. 'Look over here,' he appealed in a voice of utter incredulity. 'They've moved our coat hangers!' Other choir members wandered about the vestry trying to get their bearings. Nothing was where it used to be. There were so many new bits and pieces that the whole place was foreign. Even the cracked vestry mirror, much in demand since the advent of girls in the choir, had disappeared, and where was that venerable institution, the vestry piano that had thumped out the hymn tunes and chants for generations? Then, suddenly George gripped my arm in alarm. 'The choir photos!' he exclaimed. 'There's no room for them – all those new shelves and hangers and cupboards. How are we going to put the photos back?' 'Let's see,' I said. 'We'll go and get them now and see what we can do.'

Three or four of us juggled the photos all that Sunday between services. George kept on saying, 'There's no way,' and the tenor soloist kept on picking up the photos and putting them down again and going out into the churchyard for a smoke, and making tea for the rest of us, and saying things like, 'Vandals,' 'Criminals,' and 'You can bet the vicar's behind this.'

We worked on after evensong, taking advantage of the new state-of-the-art lighting. It was nearly midnight before we succeeded in cramming every photo somewhere, and the sight of the primrose walls had all but disappeared. None of the new cupboard doors had escaped either and we had to work hard dissuading our soprano soloist, a charming girl with a great sense of humour, from fixing a very large scowling Victorian vicar on the ceiling. George reckoned it wasn't appropriate, particularly as the state-of-the-art ceiling lighting affected the photo in such a way as to make the vicar appear as a sort of demonic figure about to spring down on the choir. But the soprano soloist still persevered with the scowling Victorian vicar and eventually, at about one o'clock in the morning, she had succeeded in placing him right next to a photo of a choir charabanc outing to the seaside in 1923, which showed the whole choir lolling in front of a disreputable-looking pub waving tankards of beer, happily unaware of the huge disapproval of the scowling Victorian vicar.

Big Hector has now moved into his enlarged

much-sought-after Victorian residence in the next village, where he is happily re-organizing the church there. He has not forgotten George's church, however. The vicar was so impressed by all his kindness and generosity in taking over the restoration work that he asked for a photograph of the benefactor to join the others in the choir vestry. This was immediately forthcoming and was very big and very dignified. The vicar left it to George to find a way of displaying it, and George left it to the soprano soloist who liked ceiling pictures.

Big Hector, the Supremo, now keeps an eye on the choir from his exalted position high amongst the state-of-the-art lighting.